Ben Sullivan

Sullivan's Stories

Bernard (Ben) Sullivan has packed a lot of activity into his long life. A born Master of Ceremonies and scion of a family which delights in story telling, he has also been greatly blessed with an eye for the funny side of life.

These lucky gifts have enabled him to garner a harvest of amusing, "different" and interesting stories over the past sixty-two years, with six years in the wartime Navy on Minesweeping Trawlers, Assault Landing Craft and Tank Landing Ships; thirty three years in the Bank of England; twenty four years as a Boxing M.C. at Wembley, the Royal Albert Hall, the Hilton on Park Lane, and the Café Royal; and forty seven years as one of London's (and therefore the World's) leading Toastmasters, officiating at the very top, with twenty three prestigious Lord Mayor's Banquets and nearly two hundred of the Great State Banquets to his credit.

Bernard's host of friends (top London Toastmasters are reported to know, personally, more people than anyone else in the World) have persuaded him to put his stories into a book. Having done this and mixed the tales well, he sincerely hopes you will enjoy them, perhaps reading one each bedtime before falling to sleep, perhaps smiling gently.

This wish could possibly be inspired by the lovely Sullivan family motto, "The Gentle hand to Victory".

Contents

1. It shouldn't happen to a nice old chief

During the early days of our marriage I made a small confession to my wife.

"Rosie" I said (I've always had this wonderful memory for names). "We Sullivans are constantly having things happen to us which don't seem to happen to other people. You've come from a nice, quiet sort of family so you may find it a bit strange at first, but I think you'll get to enjoy it. We do …".

The very next day she began to understand. It happened like this…

After a late breakfast at our honeymoon hotel in wartime Tavistock, we set off by train to Saltash, there to connect with another train to Plymouth. On arrival, we found that the only train of the day to Plymouth had gone and we were condemned to spend a few wasted hours in glamorous Saltash before we could even go back to Tavistock. A ruined day if we merely accepted it but, as I said to my adoring (and adorable) little wife, "Don't worry, sweetheart, something will happen …".

We walked over Saltash Bridge whose interesting grey paint matched the grey water which ran beneath it and then studied a couple of bomb damaged walls. Fascinating!

I was beginning to get a little worried; there seemed to be absolutely nothing to do in this one horse town, not even a café to rest in for a while.

Suddenly however, as we rounded a bend in the river, I spotted an ungainly craft in a miniature floating dock in the centre of the stream.

"Rosie" I said excitedly "that's one of those landing craft which took the special tanks in with me on "D" Day and got so badly smashed up! Funny looking things – but they did a great job!"

Just at this moment, a Chief Petty Officer, who'd been walking behind us hailed the men on the landing craft with some questions about stores.

I had an idea … "Chief", I whispered, "I wonder if you could help us. We're both in civvies but I'm a Sub-Lieutenant and my wife is a Wren and we're stuck in this town with nothing to do. Could you use your influence so that we take a look over your L.C.T?"

"Certainly I can Sir" quoth the bold and gentlemanly sailor, immediately hailing the L.C.T. to make the necessary arrangements.

The upshot of this was the despatch of a rowing boat propelled, somewhat erratically, by a Petty Officer "Chippy" or carpenter, traditionally not the Navy's best boat handlers.

The nearest landing stage was some hundred yards distant so the Chief directed the Chippy to a part of the quay wall nearer to us which had been damaged by the bombing.

"Grab that rope, Chippy," he called as our carriage bumped in an unseamanlike manner against the bombed wall.

Chippy did as he was ordered and the boat came to rest some four feet below us. So far so good but the Chief and I exchanged glances. How would a lady get down the steep bomb-damaged wall into the small unstable boat?

"Shall we leave it, Chief?" I murmured …

"No, it'll be alright, Sir" he piped up cheerily, "I'll scramble down, you lower your wife, I'll hold her ankles and guide her into the boat."

I hesitated and to tell the truth fleetingly harboured the unworthy thought "Whose honeymoon is this?" But the gallant sailor was already down in the boat calling, "Come on Sir! Lower away. I'll look after her!".

So I started to lower Wren Sullivan, then, as now, nicely plump, holding her with my crooked arms under her armpits, while the Chief took a gentle grip on her ankles.

Within seconds the weight became almost too much for me to hold! Something was going wrong! A lightning glance downwards told me all! The rowing boat had drifted away from the wall, with the stupid Chippy still holding the now almost horizontal rope, while the Chief, far from guiding Rosie's ankles was now hanging on to them like grim death.

Another calamity, not then apparent to me, but vitally important to Rosie, was that, as I'd started to lower her, her skirt had remained where it was, caught up on the jagged wall – revealing all my honeymoon suspenders and thighs to a passing liberty-boat full of vocally appreciative United States sailors.

Fast action was needed and your truly (normally more of a thinking type) supplied it. I gave one almighty tug and Rosie (minus a few cami-knickers buttons!) was back on the quay.

Without pause for a breath we both looked down. The boat was now a full six feet from the quay, the Chippy was still holding the rope and the Chief, with both feet in the boat and both hands slipping down the jagged wall, was lying chest down on top of the water.

Then, to a resounding cheer from our allies in the liberty-boat, he went under and his peaked cap floated away.

Rosie and I looked at each other, aghast. "Let's move on dear" I murmured – and we did!

We'd only gone a few yards though when we heard the dear old Chief's voice, from back in the rowing boat.

"Just go on to the landing stage Sir, where those Yanks get off, and I'll pick you up there".

We couldn't refuse and the soaking wet old sailor, who kept laughing to himself, while wringing out his handkerchief and banknotes and showing us the soggy pictures of his family, took us out to the L.C.T. for a nice lunch.

We later sent him a very classy pair of Bonsoir pyjamas which my Mother used to get on the black-market.

He was delighted but it was in truth a small reward to giving us a story to tell over all these years.

2. Get 'em 'orf

By dint of careful selection, many white lies and some luck, I do only posh jobs nowadays. Gone forever I hope, are classics like, "The Blank Street Traders Annual Punch Up", and the "Bookies Runners' Ball". Also eliminated from my list the more routine "Everyone's your boss" Jewish Weddings and the "Drink everything in sight – the Boss is paying" Firm's Christmas Parties.

Just one of the rough jobs is left and I do it (I think) out of nostalgia. Judge for yourselves.

The job is actually three jobs. A famous brewery gives its 1800 male factory employees a dinner and cabaret, 600 at a time. Always the second Tuesday, Wednesday and Thursday in January; always the same band, the same menu, the same beer (their own) the same speeches and, most important, the same type cabaret.

I start my duties by announcing "Dinner is served" in the Bar. Only the bosses are there. The workers have in the main forgone their pre-dinner drinks in order to grab a seat at a table as near as possible to the raised cabaret platform.

Having got all the lads to the tables it's "Pray silence for Grace by the Chairman". Everyone rises, pint glasses in hand, for this. Very cultured.

Then as the waitresses start to serve the first course, badly dyed blood red tomato soup, I signal the band to commence playing. They always start with "Colonel Bogey" and at the appropriate moment 640 raucous voices (including the waitresses!) join in " … and the same to you!"

I disgrace myself and scream with laughter at this.

Things then proceed fairly quietly with just the occasional roll thrown between friends and we pass through the main course, always turkey, sprouts and nearly baked potatoes, to the sweet course, always individual greasy Christmas puddings, always trapped in very thick very yellow custard.

Then to the Loyal Toast. I can best describe the boys as loyal citizens who at this stage are not terribly respectful. Then "permission to smoke" ("Those of you not already smoking may do so!")

Then to the Speech. "Pray silence for your Chairman" (a famous beer baron). His speech usually takes about one minute. "The football team did well this year, we lost £400,000 on your bloody strike – hope you have a happy evening. I'll now hand you over to the Toastmaster".

"Gentlemen", I then say (on each of the three nights year after year) "It is now ten past eight. The cabaret will start at eight-thirty. The toilets are there (pointing right) and there (pointing left). Any gentlemen going through that door (pointing straight ahead of me) will not be re-admitted." (The door in question is near the cabaret girls' changing room and there's been a bit of trouble in former years!)

At eight-thirty precisely (the congregation won't wait longer) the Cabaret starts. I jump up on the stage and amid a chorus of "Get 'em 'orf" (which I of course ignore), introduce the first act. "Jean Belmont presents London's Premier Floor Show – The Gayetimers".

The band (a tip top London outfit) burst into a gay tune and on dance the girls (how young they look or is it me getting older?). One grabs the mike and belts out a quick and lively song, the others float gracefully around kicking their legs up and winking at the by now easily excited beer makers. This first spot lasts about three minutes – "Thank you Jean. Thank you the Gayetimers! Don't worry gentlemen, they'll be back soon."

The second turn is usually a limbo dancer. (Last year it was Claudie Cariba a supple young lady with an enormous bust which, in that uninhibited assembly gave rise to much comment – some of it highly amusing).

To the throbbing of oil drums she does her stuff, edging under lower and yet lower bars (reminding me once again of the old story of the Brixton Council putting an extra piece of wood to cover the gap under the door in the public lavatories because the limbo dancers were getting in free!) and generally getting the boys even more excited. Then she's off. "Thank you Claudie. Happy trip back to Jamaica". (Brixton really!)

A brief return of the Gayetimers, with a nice three-minutes of colourful flowing (respectable) movement and then it's time for me to introduce, " – from the land of waving palms (I assume palms grow in Turkey), full of Eastern promise … Serena!"

The belly dancer mounts the step, everything quivering and bells a jingling and one can actually see beery eyes lighting up through the haze of smoke round the hall. "Get 'em 'orf" they roar.

As if to please them, but she was going to do it anyway, she throws off a couple of veils; then to throbbing music, dances the exciting Belly-dance.

Strange as it seems, I watch the drummer during this performance. An English chap, with a rather flat head, very fair hair and staring eyes, his job is to provide rolls of the drum matching the movements of the dancer so closely as to become mesmerised. A rapport builds up between these two strangers, some ten yards apart, and they begin to seem as one.

At one time when she sits on her heels, lowers her back to the floor and starts her abdomen moving in and out, up and down to his drum rolls, he looks like a raving lunatic. Head thrust forward, eyes bolting, neck tendons stretched like whipcord, he reminds me of an arrow just about to be launched.

Suddenly Serena subsides, whacked out. They do work hard these girls.

"Thank you Serena – have a little lay down in my changing-room (all the old corn!) And now gentlemen, a chance for you to join the Brewers' Choir in full throated unison – singing the old songs played by Ruth and Betty".

On come two rather stout, elderly ladies both playing accordions. Not at all like the younger ladies in the show, but they help to balance things by leading the boys in all the old songs. They are received surprisingly well and after ten minutes bow off to thunderous applause, with only a few "Get 'em 'orfs".

"Thank you Ruth and Betty – we still love you" I call over the microphone. "A couple of real troupers eh gentlemen?"

Then a dramatic roll on the drums and I announce to a suddenly tense audience, "Gentlemen fasten your seat belts, for the star of the evening – Mademoiselle Sigi".

Yes, it's the Stripper. She's beautiful and disdainful and she teases them very artistically for at least five minutes before she gets down to the serious business of removing her clothing. A couple of the boys can't stand it, attempt to climb on to the stage to help and are removed quite roughly by commissionaires. Mlle. Sigi shows not the slightest interest in them. She even ignores the band-leader's repeated "It's a fella, I tell yer".

Then off comes this, and that. A bit of bending and stretching with bits of anatomy popping out and back – fascinating.

Suddenly, everything's off and this gorgeous figure is striding round the stage, throwing feathers to the now wild-eyed brewers.

I'm always immensely tickled when near the end of her performance and whilst gliding round the stage in the altogether, gracefully waving her arms, Mlle. Sigi slightly inclines her left wrist inwards so that as she tosses her head she can see the time on her watch. I can almost hear her saying to herself "I'll give these mugs another minute!"

4

Then it's all over. She comes off the stage where I'm waiting, eyes nearly averted, ready with her cloak. A deep breath or two and it's "Thank you gentlemen, see you next year ... ".

When I get home my wife as usual asks me how the job went. "It's my roughest of the year, dear" I say. "When they ring up for next year" she suggests brightly and wickedly, "shall I tell them you've already been booked for something else?"

"No" – I say as casually as I'm able, "we'd better leave it – there's not much work around in January ...".

Besides that – I love those old tyme songs

---

3. I never knew that!

One evening at the Mansion House, the Guest of Honour at a Livery Company's Banquet was the Chairman of British Petroleum Ltd.

The toast to 'The Guests' was proposed by a member of the Court of Common Council who was extremely well versed in City lore. He gave a very nice and thoughtful speech, mentioning each of the official guests and relating an appropriate and short anecdote about him. Coming lastly to the Guest of Honour (who was to reply to the Toast) he mentioned that B.P.'s new skyscraper, then being built in Ropemaker Street, would be the tallest building in the Square Mile. It was also to be so broadly based, he said, as to cover what formerly had been an old City thoroughfare known as Tenter Street, where the 'Tenters' (makers of tenting and tarpaulins) lived and worked.

As the Guest of Honour nodded agreement to this, the speaker went on to say that, in the old days, the workers used to stretch and measure the tarpaulins in the roadway, where hooks were fixed at regular lengths and widths. The tenters, of course, could wend their way along and across the road in perfect safety, but a stranger walking there, especially after dark in those badly lit times, would have to be very careful. He would in fact be 'walking on tenterhooks'.

'And this,' the speaker confirmed to a now fascinated Guest of Honour (and Toastmaster) 'is the origin of the expression, "I was on tenterhooks," used to describe moments of acute apprehension'.

4. Mild green fairy boxer

The one minute interval between rounds at boxing matches should be a time of rest and recuperation for the boxers. My personal opinion is that their interests would best be served if they could just be sat down and merely be encouraged to breathe deeply, and relax.

In practice, however, when they stagger back to their corners, the boxers are slammed down on to their stools and subjected to some of the most un-relaxing treatment possible. One of the Seconds immediately smashes a soaking wet sponge into the poor boxer's face and then rubs and squeezes it all over his head; another grabs his abdomen and endeavours to pull it up into his chest. Stinging, hurtful coagulators are jammed into open cuts on eyebrows; Vaseline is plastered liberally over facial protrusions and the trainer screams advice ('move away from 'is right 'and') and encouragement ('you 'ad 'im worried then – 'ee fort 'eed killed ya!'). Then the bell clangs and the warrior returns to the centre of the ring, thankful, no doubt, to get back to facing just one opponent.

We have our variations, though. One night at Wembley when Mark Harris of Guyana was boxing Colin Jones of Wales (a terrific puncher) for the Welterweight Championship of the Commonwealth, I saw him totter back to his corner at the end of the first round, pleased at the chance of a rest from Colin's hammer blows.

As he sat down heavily, his Seconds tore a new sponge from its plastic container, plunged it into their bucket of water and thrust it into his face. Mark's jet black countenance immediately took on an expression of surprise. So did the faces of all those around him – for his head had been transformed into a pillow of foaming suds. The nearest we'd seen to a boxer in a bonnet.

Fast action was needed! Back went the sponge into the bucket and again it was banged into poor Mark's face. This time the result was sensational – Mark's head looked like an advertisement for Fairy Liquid with two very puzzled, rolling, Guyanan eyes peering out at us.

Then came the bell. Mark's face was given a rapid wipe-over with a dry towel and then, with soap bubbles still popping in his thick fuzzy hair, he sprang forward to resume his battle with Colin.

A ringside spectator provided me with the answer to our little mystery.

'MC!' he called, throwing me the small plastic bag which the Guyanan Seconds had dropped, 'Have a look at that'.

I did, and on its side was printed:-

JONES HARDWARE STORE, WEMBLEY
SOAP IMPREGNATED CAR SPONGE

5. Rank bad manners

I've always liked the story of the brash, interfering cockney cab-driver who, when taking a Duchess and her young daughter through the West-End, heard the girl say "Mamma, why are those ladies standing on the corner?" and the Duchess tactfully murmur "They're waiting for their husbands, dear".

"Tell the kid the troof Missus" he interrupted and proceeded to do this himself, in explicit terms.

The young girl listened, wide-eyed and puzzled. "But what happens Mamma, if the prostitutes have babies?"

"Where do you think we get our taxi-drivers from…" Was the Duchess's tight-lipped rejoinder.

I thought of this tale at the conclusion of a Cricketing Dinner at the London Hilton one evening, when I was asked by the President to escort the Guest of Honour from the banqueting hall, through the foyer, to his car.

As the Guest of Honour was no less than His Royal Highness the Prince Philip, Duke of Edinburgh, there were lots of hotel guests, mainly Americans, anxious for a glance at or even a quick word or handshake with the great man. Nevertheless, by gently steering a path through (I think my crimson coat helps a lot on such occasions) I was able to get him, and his bodyguard, a Chief Superintendent of Police, out to the royal carriage with the minimum of fuss.

The royal carriage that night was an all-electric Bedford van and, after nicely thanking me for my efforts, Prince Philip climbed into the driver's seat, leaving the Chief to settle in the passenger's one.

At that very moment a taxi drew alongside, double parking, to allow the fare to alight. This of course prevented the Prince from driving off but he just smiled …

The innocent fare settled his bill without hassle, exchanged some pleasantry or other with the cabbie and moved off into the hotel, and Philip was still smiling patiently.

We fully expected the cabbie to move off then, ready to pick up another rich tourist but, instead, he turned off his engine, took a black cloth bag from the inner side of his seat and very slowly began to count from it, his takings for the evening.

The realisation that this might take too much time for comfort, or perhaps, more importantly, for security, flashed with equal speed upon the Prince, the detective and the toastmaster.

As I was at pavement level, I thought I'd try to sort out this minor traffic jam.

"Cabbie" I said politely, "could you go back a bit, or move out please – you're holding up the chap on your left".

"Can't you see I'm counting me blee'nt money?" he growled.

"Cabbie" I hissed, more firmly, "hurry up. The bloke you're holding up is Prince Philip, the Queen's husband".

" xxxx the Queen's 'usband" came the less than patriotic reply.

I, a gentle and respectful Royalist, was struck dumb by this turn of events – but help was at hand …

"Leave this to me, old chap" came a quiet voice. It was the Chief Superintendent who must have moved like greased lightening from the passenger's seat, round the front of the van, the taxi and me.

A few very quiet words were murmured to the cabbie – who immediately dropped his bag of money, started the engine and rocketed away.

"Good night old boy" smiled the Chief to me, climbing back into the van.

"Good night" chuckled Prince Philip driving the electric van silently away into the London night …

I shall never forget that little incident. Just what did the Chief say to that nasty son-of-a-bitch?

6. Lionel – gents hairdresser

The "gents hairdresser" at the Royal Exchange, one Lionel, is quite a character. A superb craftsman, he probably keeps in immaculate condition the silvery locks of more distinguished Englishmen than any other man in the profession.

One evening after he'd done his best with my thatch and was trimming my 'murderer's eyebrows', he thrust an invitation card into my hands.

It requested the pleasure of my company for cocktails, in the shop, the following Monday to celebrate his 25 years in the City. "I know you don't drink", he said "and I know you're busy in the evenings, but I'd like you to come. You're one of my oldest and most decrepit customers".

"I'll come" I said. "I'd like to see a Cocktail Party in a barber's shop".

"You'll enjoy it" he said "and I'll get some Orangeade in". I thought for a moment – "I'm bringing my Toastmaster's outfit for a function late on Monday evening. Would you like me to come to the shop in my red coat and announce the guests as they arrive?"

"That's what I was after, really!" confirmed the crafty old crop clipper and he screamed with laughter. I did too (as soon as he'd moved his razor from my throat) because it was so preposterous, so ridiculous. A cocktail party in a barber's shop! Guests announced at the cash desk!

"You're mad" I chided him.

"Yes, b… potty", he said "… you know how many are coming?"

"Go on, tell me".

"Five hundred", he chortled!

It was crazy but it was going to be different! I'd go.

Came the night and I reported at the shop some ten minutes before take-off. Lionel had removed the big barber's chairs and the place looked quite spacious. I reckoned it would take at least eighty people!

"Right SIR" I said to Lionel. ("Stop crawling" he said). "Will you please stand there to receive your guests. I'll announce their names and if you can give each of them just a quick handshake and only a couple of words, that will save a queue building up in the street".

"Right-o, cock" says Lionel "You're the boss".

"That's right Lionel" came an amused voice from the doorway, "do as you're told, for once". It was our first visitor – The Chairman of the Stock Exchange.

I announced this distinguished guest in precisely the manner I'd often done at Guildhall and all three of us howled with laughter.

A great start to the evening!

Guests then began to arrive faster than I could announce or Lionel could receive them. He was great – a born host with a rare gift of greeting people warmly, giving them a quick insult and a laugh and then passing them on quickly. Would that all Chairmen and Presidents were like Lionel!

If I tell you that the first twenty guests included the Chairman of Lloyds, the Governor of the Bank of England and a former Lord Mayor of London, you'll think I'm kidding; but it's true. They and the bankers, brokers, company chairmen and aldermen who followed, formed as distinguished a company as you'd find at any Embassy reception!

And they were all laughing; laughing as they queued on the pavement in a faint drizzle of rain, laughing as they were announced, and laughing whilst they supped champagne in the cash desk, over a wash-hand basin or crushed against the hair-oil shelves.

I "clicked in" four hundred and sixty three distinguished city men into one barber's shop and they never stopped laughing. I think it was the damned check of the whole thing that tickled their fancies.

It probably couldn't have been done anywhere in the world but the City of London with those highly intelligent, very well mannered and tolerant gentlemen who are 'something in the City'.

At the end of this great 'laugh-in' Lionel said, "We agreed, no fee. Right?"

"Right" I said, firmly.

"Have I ever refused a tip from you?" he asked.

"Of course not" I laughed.

"Well you can't refuse one from me" he said, and thrust a sealed envelope into my hand.

I later found it contained more money than I would have charged as a fee! That, I thought epitomised the whole crazy evening. The barber tipped the customer!!

With many others I look forward with glee to Lionel's next party; but with City rates now so astronomically high and the modern chaps only coming in for a haircut about once in nine weeks, I doubt we'll see another.

SUPPORT YOUR CITY BARBER GENTLEMEN

7. Boxing writers' dinner

At the Boxing Writers' Dinner each January there assemble some three hundred rather tough guys; boxers, ex boxers, promoters, managers trainers, referees and the like.

There are always two Guests of Honour, one a person well known to the public through politics or television, who will be the principal speaker of the evening and the other the young lad whom the Boxing Writers have elected "The Most Promising Young Boxer of 19 ..." (the previous year).

A few years ago the principal speaker was a very famous, rather portly star of stage, screen and television and the boxer was a young Cockney boy called Johnny.

At the pre-banquet cocktails everybody made a great and sincere fuss over young Johnny (who was a fine boxer and a very likeable chap) and he enjoyed himself hugely. An eighteen year old, surrounded by his boxing heroes and many other famous people all congratulating him!

During dinner, however, I noticed that Johnny, in his top-table position of honour on the Chairman's left, was <u>looking decidedly</u> less cheerful. The Chairman had engaged in deep middle-aged conversation with the portly star on his right thus unwittingly neglecting Johnny. The Vice Chairman, on Johnny's left, was just as deeply embroiled with a famous comedian on his left. A top table position when it's your first West End banquet, you've finished a course, no one is talking to you and you're a Cockney kid of eighteen is one of the loneliest places on earth.

A Cockney kid myself, I decided to try to help. A quiet note to the Chairman in the hope that he would, after a suitable pause, turn casually back to Johnny, seemed to be the answer.

I therefore as politely as I could, broke into the conversation between the Chairman and the portly star, saying to the latter "Sorry to interrupt Sir, I have a message for the Chairman" and showing the Chairman a small piece of paper on which I'd written "Young Johnny looks lonely".

His reaction surprised me; an absolutely lightning glance and the words "Oh yes! Yes! I agree". Just that – and then he hurriedly continued his conversation with the star.

I was really puzzled as I made my way back to my table; why that lightning glance and why was the Chairman still ignoring Johnny?

I looked at the note again. Could the Chairman have misunderstood it? A slight suspicion began to dawn as I looked at the last word; could he have mistaken my written N for a V?

Johnny was <u>still</u> looking lonely so I printed the word "LONELY" under its written form on the note, interrupted the star again (he was annoyed this time) and said to the Chairman, pointing to the PRINTED word, "This message again, Sir. Did you understand?"

"My God" he cried, and whirled round to talk to Johnny.

I've often wondered what went through the Chairman's mind as he flashed me that first significant glance. I thank he made the very quick assumption that, in the rugged, cauliflower-eared assembly he had a suspect Toastmaster who not only had developed a crush on the junior Guest of Honour but had such a compulsion to tell someone about it, that he interrupted the Chairman, right there in the centre of the top-table to do so.

8. Get knotted

Within a few weeks of Victory in Europe my ship, H. M. Landing Ship, Tank, 77, based in the Mediterranean, was engaged in a great variety of jobs such as closing down bases on the Greek Islands, repatriating refugees and delivering prisoners of war. We sometimes even purchased cigarettes from Greek tobacco growers and sold them to cigarette starved Italians – although I'm not sure the Navy were aware of this chore!

Some of the tasks were pretty grim; once, in the absence of the Sick Berth Attendant (in hospital with 'Disease caught ashore!') I had to look after 20 very pregnant, very sea-sick women non-stop for twelve nightmarish hours but others were as thrilling as minesweeping the Venetian canals with our small landing craft or as peaceful as a pre-war Mediterranean cruise.

One of the peaceful tasks was the moving of a group of the famous United States Construction Battalions (the 'Seabees') from one island to another so that they could build airstrips. There was to be a chain of these from Europe to the Far East, so that small fighter planes could fly to the Pacific (where they were needed against the Japanese) in a series of short hops.

The Seabees were all hefty great chaps famous for working long hours at great speed. They looked on their days on board the ship as a period of rest and relaxation, spending their time sunbathing, playing cards, washing smalls and so on, on our two hundred foot long deck.

CARRICK BEND

One balmy day as I was just finishing a four hour trick as officer-of-the-watch, I contemplated the scene ahead of me. A sea really looking like glass; an absolutely cloudless sky and a lovely warm sun. On the deck, some Seabees relaxing; no fears about U-boats or hostile aircraft … just a peaceful cruise.

A movement on the f'castle caught my eye. One of the Seabees had washed his classy champagne-coloured safari suit, tied it to one of our heaving lines and thrown it outboard to trail in the frictional wake (the one running down the side of the ship) so as to rinse it, in one of the most beautiful ways possible, in fast flowing sea-water.

Unfortunately, however, as I could see from my vantage point in the bridge, the line wasn't long enough and the clothing was hanging some six inches above the water. For all the rinsing it was getting he might as well have hung it on the mast!

What was he waiting for? A storm? Somehow it worried me. It was so inefficient. Why didn't the damn fool pull it up?

Suddenly, the 'watch' was over. My relief Sub-Lieutenant 'Bash' Hill had arrived on the bridge…

"Ah! Bash" I said, "we're to keep her on a course of 120 at 12 knots and tell the old man as soon as we sight the island. O.K?" And I started to leave…

"Hold it, son" said Bash, who normally liked a little chat at the change-over of a watch "what's the hurry? Got a bird down there, or something?"

"No" I smiled, "I'm just going down to tell that bloke (pointing to the f'castle) about his clothes. They're not even touching the water". Bash looked at the still dry clothing hanging over the bow and sighed. He knew me well…

"Why don't you just mind your own business" he said, wearily, "leave it, go and have your tea".

"They won't mind, Bash" I countered, "I'm only trying to help. You watch". And with the bright face of someone about to do a good turn, I hurried down from the bridge and then forward to the cheerful group of big chaps on the f'castle.

"Afternoon, gentlemen" I greeted them, "whose washing's that hanging over the side?"

A nice looking chap, clad only in some rather jazzy underclothes, stepped forward, slightly apprehensive.

"It's mine, Sir" he said apologetically, "I hope I've not done anything wrong".

"Of course not" I answered reassuringly, "I just wanted to tell you it's not touching the water".

"The rope's not long enough, Sir" he said, simply.

"Why don't you bend it to the other heaving line" I suggested, my eyes pointing to the other line, lying on the deck.

"Bend it, Sir?"

"I'm sorry, that's Navy for 'join it'. Tie the two heaving lines together".

"Oh! I didn't dare do that Sir; I don't trust my knots".

I was surprised at this and said so, finishing with "I thought you boys in the Seabees use as many knots as we do".

A chorus of denial came from the interested little group of big fellows who had gathered round.

"Give me the two heaving lines, lads" I said. "I'll join them for you and I'll teach you a smashing knot – it'll be useful in your business".

Willing hands passed the two lines to me and a fairly big crowd gathered round. Bash, on the bridge, started shaking his head…

"Now gents" I started, "this is how you tie the CARRICK BEND. It's a fabulous knot for joining two pieces of rope. It never jams, whatever the strain, so you can undo it easily when you want to. It also forms a nice round shape so that you can pass it round a winch without causing a stoppage.

They all craned forward; a very attentive audience. (I loved it).

A few flourishing and, though I say it myself, expert movements and the two lines were joined.

"There you are gents" I purred, modestly ignoring their admiring glances, "now watch this". And after pulling the knot very tightly, nonchalantly loosened it.

I seem to remember a small round of applause at that stage.

Repetition as you know is the most efficient way of teaching a simple skill. I therefore repeated the demonstration perhaps six times, finishing on a high note of audience participation by asking two eighteen stone giants to pull on the ropes, tug-of-war style, so that the knot looked impossibly jammed. Then with a seamanlike flick of the wrist, loosened it.

All really good stuff, marred only slightly by the expression on Bash's face. Even at two hundred feet I could discern his 'disgusted' look.

"Gentlemen", I now called to my hundred or so audience. "I'll have to go. Let's join the lines for the last time and then get those clothes rinsed properly".

The two lines were then joined with a Carrick Bend and one of the Seabees went to throw the clothes outboard.

"Hold it!" I called urgently, and (with a teacher's patient smile) continued, "You've not tied the other end on to the rail. Let me help".

Then with practised hand I tied the loose end of the second line to the guard rail using a Clove Hitch and Extra Turn.

"Now you can throw them."

Throw them he did and having heard the satisfying splash I started back toward the bridge for tea. I felt I deserved it. I'd done my little bit towards Anglo-American relations; helped some poor stranger and given quite a little show. What could please a 'ham' more?

Bash still didn't seem too impressed. He was, in fact, looking over the starboard side as if watching something slide by. His head turned further and further aft…

Suddenly, the whole ship vibrated for a few seconds. A noise very familiar to Landing Craft and Landing Ship men … something had momentarily become entangled in the propellers.

Bash turned back slowly, shaking his head in disbelief and at that moment I knew. In a terrible flash I knew. The damned Carrick Bend had come undone, the poor chap's Safari suit had been swept down the side right into the twin propellers which had then torn it into tiny pieces!!

I looked at my victim, standing there in his underclothes (perhaps for the remainder of the voyage) and could see that the truth was dawning on him, too.

"I'm terribly sorry, old boy" I stuttered humbly and then (in probably my most sensible action that day) burst into peals of laughter. I just couldn't help it. Those clothes had been hanging quite safely until I'd poked my big nose in; now, after an expert demonstration in the art of British knots, they were sinking in tiny pieces towards the bottom of the sea.

The laughter saved the day and perhaps my neck! The Seabees started to see the funny side and the deck began to resound with their guffaws. Several even joined me (and 'Underclothes') in the luxury of tears of pure joy.

I promised the poor chap I would speak to his officer, at tea, and try to get him a new suit – paying for it myself, if this proved necessary.

In the event, amid further joyous uproar in the wardroom, the officer said that the ripping to pieces of a soldier's uniform could only be regarded as the work of an enemy; consequently the suit could be replaced free.

It all worked out so well – a great laugh and a story to tell over the years – that I was asked to try it again next trip. But supported by Bash, who said his nerves couldn't stand it, I declined.

9. The pinching plenipotentiary

I've looked after many "book launching" parties in my time, and they are nice occasions.

The publisher usually invites a mixed bag of booksellers, critics and television commentators to come along 'to meet the author' and if possible persuade a few well known peers, politicians etc. to add lustre to the cluster.

Copies of the book which is launched are normally displayed on various small tables around the hall and are sometimes presented to guests. The number so presented naturally varies with the price of the book.

One night at a great hotel a heavy tome was being launched which traced the history of the benefits bestowed by the British on their Colonies; peace, justice, roads, education, health services etc. It was about the size of the Stock Exchange Year Book. (Perhaps we didn't treat them so badly, after all).

As could be expected, we had several High Commissioners and Ministers present, together with many former Governors General. One of the Ministers seemed to be extremely young for such a position and it turned out he was the son of some diplomat. He'd been educated at Oxbridge, spoke like a pre-war B.B.C. announcer and dressed as though he'd stepped out of Harrods' window.

When I announced him, "The First Minister of …" he swept in, all teeth and talk. I frankly can't bear his type, but the hosts gave him a cordial welcome and he mixed easily enough with the other guests.

After some fifteen minutes of cocktails and canapés he left the room with a friend as flashy as himself. Each was carrying a copy of the book which was being launched…

"Goodnight, gentlemen", I said politely, thinking they were leaving early perhaps to attend another party on the Diplomatic circuit.

"Oh, I'm not going" said our hero, in that terribly posh voice, "I'm just seeing my friend orf".

He returned a little later and gave me a big smile; it was so friendly that I nearly missed noting he'd come back empty-handed; possibly his friend had kindly agreed to take both books home…

Five minutes later the Honourable the First minister passed out of the room carrying another copy of the book. "Goodnight Sir" I said, confident that this <u>was</u> the going of him. I was wrong though, for he said cheerily, "Oh no, man, I'll be back soon".

In view of my deepening (though incredible) suspicion that the Honourable Minister was being dishonourable, this seemed to me more of a threat than a promise. There were after all some ten books still scattered round the small tables!

"Madam" I called quietly to the organiser, "could I have a quick word". She came over.

"Are you giving away copies of the book, Madam?"

"What, at £12.50 a copy!" She exclaimed. "You must be joking".

"Well, the Minister for Blank has had three", I warned "and I am sure he's coming back for more".

"What?" she gasped and made a quick count, "My God, what can we do?"

"Well, we can't very well stop him at the door and call him a thief", I said, "Not a Minister! What about collecting all the books and stacking them behind the bar?"

She looked doubtful.

"Come on Madam" I advised briskly "he'll be back soon", and so saying I scooped up two books from the nearest table. That did it. Soon all ten copies were stacked behind the bar and the Italian barman was given strict instructions not to let any go without permission from the organiser.

Not a moment too soon. I just had time to get back to the door before young Raffles arrived. Was it my imagination or did he seem more purposeful? Was this to be a last big swoop?

I really believe that was the case because he made his way through the guests, arms slightly to the fore (as though about to lift?) straight toward the first table.

His surprise at seeing it bare, was complete. He stopped short and did a "double take". He then turned and moved urgently toward another table; and another and another. All empty.

"That's done the bath bun", I said to myself.

He didn't give in that easily, however; his eyes were everywhere and soon they rested on the stack of books behind the bar.

He strolled over and in a voice casually authoritative, said to the barman "Would you pass me my two books from the top, please".

Such is the power of a confident instruction that the barman started to get them! Even I, who'd been convinced that we had a pinching plenipotentiary among us, began to waver – but I stiffened in time.

"May I help Sir?" I enquired.

"I'm just collecting my books" he explained.

"There must be some mistake, Sir, those ten are reserved for Lord …" I lied. "Where did you leave your's, Sir?"

"On that table" he pointed "and I saw them being moved over to here".

What a beautiful liar! He was out of the room at the time of the removal! I was outclassed – just a poor honest banker.

"Madam" I called desperately to the organiser, "could you help this gentleman? He thinks his books are mixed up with Lord …s".

"Yes" he explained, "there are two of my books there".

The cool cheek. The tenacity – he was talking to the organiser! The owner of the damned books.

But bless English girls! She beat him just as they beat us when they are roused. "There are ten books left" she said, very distinctly, "and they belong to Lord…".

Raffles knew he was defeated (if getting away with three £12.50 books is a defeat). He therefore contented himself with witty conversation and plenty of drinks for the next forty five minutes – and was the last guest to depart.

And, even though we saw him leave empty handed, we counted those books again!

---

10. Bye, bye, dolly

Having completed my labours in a London Embassy at a cocktail reception given for a Canadian Prime Minister, I asked him for his autograph for my collection and went off in search of the caterer, who was to pay me.

I found him near a bar which had been set up in the lounge. He was very busy and as I was in no hurry, I stood about four yards from him, and waited.

He noticed me immediately, however, and knew instinctively that I was there for my money.

"Can I see you in a minute Chief", he said, "I'm a bit tied up".

"No hurry", I said.

"Have a drink while you're waiting", he suggested. "Dolly", he called to a homely, sweet, white haired, opened-faced barmaid who was washing some glasses, "Give the Toastmaster a drink".

Not wishing Dolly to have to stop work, dry her hands, etc. for something I could easily do for myself, I said "Don't worry, Doll, I'll do it".

I picked up a small bottle of fruit juice and, amid a quiet chorus from Dolly and the other waitresses of, "Ave something stronger than that" poured it, with a flourish into a large glass.

"I'll surprise you girls", I said, reaching for one of two large water jugs on the bar just in front of Dolly, "even fruit juice is a bit strong for me".

They looked suitably impressed and so, with an even bigger flourish, I poured a lot of water on to my small fruit juice.

"Ladies!" I cried, raising the glass, "Your very good health!"

With that, teetotaller-like, I took a large gulp. It was awful! Took my breath away and sucked my cheeks in so far that they met inside my mouth!

"Strewth" I gasped, "That's poisonous. Watch it. There's something wrong with that water. It's … it's (as my paralysed taste buds began to function again) it's GIN!"

"Shut up" snarled Dolly.

So I did the sporting thing and kept my mouth shut. My eyes and ears remained wide open however and, whilst the caterer was paying me, his back to the bar, I laughed to myself when I heard sweet Dolly's motherly voice say, "If no one wants this water I'll empty it", and watched as the crafty old crook wended her way to the kitchen with her two large jugs of gin.

---

11. Not like the 9.15 from Petts Wood

Boarding a London bus at about 5.30 one morning, my Dad (the best story teller I've ever known) joined the noisy gang of cockney charladies and other early morning characters on the upper deck and, as on many previous occasions settled down to enjoy a cigarette and good company

The chatter around him was in the main as uninhibited and amusing at usual but within a few moments he discerned an element, nay a whiff, of tensions and noted that some of the girls were staring with undisguised hostility at a fellow passenger, a thin, extremely miserable looking man.

Dad's attention was almost immediately distracted by the sound of heavy boots stamping up the stairway, a snatch of song, a cheerful shout of "Mawnin Lydis" and the traditional cry of "'Ave yer fez reddee, pleez . . . . ."

It was of course the conductor, who them proceeded jovially and casually towards the front, issuing tickets, taking money, exchanging mock insults with old customers and rendering short bursts of "Sweet Adeline."

As he neared the thin man, however, the singing stopped, abruptly, and the conductor gave an almighty sniff . . . . .

'Oo's passed a motion?" he roared. (or words to that effect)

"I 'ave" said the thin man.

Heads swivelled round. Faces showed disgust, amusement . . . . . pity.

"Ar fink you really 'ave, yer dirty bleeder" said the conductor.

"I 'ave" came the sad confirmation.

A chorus of condemnation swelled on the upper deck: "Chuck 'im orf," "Wouldya believe it?," "An nitt nice, eh?," "Get orf," "Oppit" . . . . .

"I ain't gettin orf," came the defiant response, "ar got one more stop an its righ artside ma firm. I ain't gonna walk all that way like this - an ar've paid me fare!"

There was a certain logic in this and Dad could see the conductor's neck muscles twitching as he wrestled with the problem before making a momentous decision . . . . . "Clang" went the bus on its short but by now highly charged journey.

Arrival at the firm's gates was marked by a sudden deathly hush. Heads turned accusingly, expectantly and the thin man rose very carefully, shuffled along the bus, down the stairs, across the pavement and then extremely slowly into the works yard.

His every step was monitored closely by some fifty fascinated people, crowding the windows of the top deck, including the conductor who, Dad felt, summed it all up by shaking his head and murmuring "Stone me blind . . . . . the poor sod . . . . ." before clanging the bell.

Speaking of Dad's memorable early morning journey to work reminds me of one of mine . . . . . Before the war I worked on Smithfield Market and used to start business there at 4.00 a.m. As there was no public transport available I walked from Islington to Smithfield every morning. Enjoyed it too . . . . .

One morning, as I turned the blind corner of a high wall round the local graveyard, I bumped full tilt into a policeman who was "just standing there".

At that hour (3 a.m.) and in that location one didn't welcome such sudden encounters and I was shaken from my normal and humble respect for the Law.

"What the blankety-blank you wanna stand right on the edge for" I gasped. "You frightened the life outa me!"

The copper's reply has lived with me for sixty five years.

"Wot am ar s'poster do cos you're coming rahn the cawner?" he hissed, "Blow me blee'nt whissool?"

12. The rise and fall of the Sun

I felt honoured, some years ago, at being invited to perform at the Talk of the Town. Treading in the footsteps of Bruce Forsythe and Frankie Vaughan? Alas no. I was to be Toastmaster at the party launching a new newspaper – the Sun.

This new publication, which was to replace the poor old "Daily Herald", was to be run by Mr Hugh Cudlipp (now Lord Cudlipp) a man for whom I have a high regard. He had, it seemed, invited the whole of the Fleet Street establishment to the launch – and what a tough, sharp, hard-drinking bunch of cookies they were …

On arrival I was given a sheaf of instructions covering the whole of the day's operations, every opening and closing of stage curtains, every use of spotlights, lifts, screens, backdrops, microphones. This was frightening but then it emerged that I was merely to persuade all guests on arrival to tramp up to the "circle" for cocktails, get them back to the "stalls" when it was time for lunch and then, when lunch was finished, to introduce the Presentation by intoning, from the wings of the stage, the Sun's slogan … "A newspaper for our time – for the people of our time".

This was to be the signal for the stage curtains to open, dramatically, revealing a screen on which the word "SUN" would appear.

Then Hugh Cudlipp would take over and from a raised Presidential stand in front of the stage welcome his guests and, with the aid of a succession of slides, tell them all about his new daily.

Mr Cudlipp, a man who likes things to be done properly, drilled us quite ruthlessly for about an hour before the arrival of the guests. Everything had to be perfect and the change from convivial lunch to commercial presentation had to be dramatic, eye-catching and riveting … Quite right too, because the Presentation was being made to hard-boiled rivals.

It really was tough. I, for instance, had to rehearse "A newspaper of our time for the people of our time" some twenty times before achieving the right mix of clarity, vibrancy and authority to satisfy our Host. Then the sound technician had to move the microphone on Mr Cudlipp's stand up and down, a centimetre at a time before fixing it in the perfect position for his voice. Then the electrician had to paint the light bulb on the stand to dim it sufficiently – and so on.

Then the guests arrived. There was of course no difficulty in persuading these boys to visit the bar and strangely, only slight difficulty in getting them away from it, for lunch. And being well wined and dined they were, it was hoped in a receptive mood, ready to watch the Presentation. So far, so good.

Mr Cudlipp mounted his stand, placed his notes on the lectern, switched on his painted, dim light and then, with a thin baton gave three very gentle taps on the microphone mounted exactly 6⅜ inches above the lectern. Perfect.

Absolutely on cue, every light in the theatre then dimmed and, thrilled to the marrow, I did my Laurence Olivier bit " … A newspaper of our time … for the people of our time".

The stage curtains swished open dramatically and, amid a chorus of cynical laughter, the first slide came up.

It said "NUS"

Over the microphone came a strangled sound, which could it have been unscrambled, was probably a terrible oath.

Three urgent taps of the baton and the offending slide vanished to the right, reappearing nervously as "SUN" – and then dissolving in an oily mess! The slide had burned out.

There was now an uproar of cruel laughter from all Mr Cudlipp's rivals in the audience. They were absolutely delighted at his discomfort.

"Put the lights on. Put the dammed lights on", he said.

The electrician, probably assuming that it would be his last ever duty for Mr Cudlipp, put all the lights on.

Mr Cudlipp then faced his tormentors. He could have ranted and raved at them. He could have apologised and blamed his staff. He did none of these things. He just said "If I find the bastard the Daily Express has sent over here to sabotage us, I'll have his guts for garters".

The jeers turned to cheers and amid great and sympathetic applause, we started again. Inspired by this natural leader of men, we made no more mistakes and gave a perfect presentation.

Footnote:
That version of the "Sun" unfortunately only lasted about three months before going broke. Then another chap brought out a new "Sun" which runs profitably to this day. He, in my unimportant opinion, was a lesser man than Cudlipp, but he'd obviously learned one great truth about selling newspapers to the British public. It seems that, each day on Page three, you must …

13. The silly bitch

Things are not always what they seem to be. Thus at your Association's Dinner Dance the jolly band-leader might well be a tax-collector by day. The sly cabaret magician might in turn be an honest bank clerk, the thoughtful photographer a computer programmer and your helpful Toastmaster, an exchange controller!

One noble knight (let us call him 'Sir Charles') the President of a great National Society, suffered a nasty moment one evening because of this moonlighting aspect of our social merry-go-round.

He and his lady arrived at a famous banqueting suite the requisite half hour before the reception was due to start so that he could give his instructions, ask any questions and order wines for himself and guests. They were a high class couple; she a very good looking woman, beautifully turned out, and he an upright, distinguished man wearing the Sash and Star of a famous Order of Chivalry. They were very friendly but with a natural dignity which gave them great authority. Definitely a Knight and his Lady.

"Hello Toastmaster", said her Ladyship, "Been to any famous banquets lately? You told us some good stories last year …"

"Well I did that one on Monday, my Lady, when Mr Roy Jenkins said that his next Budget would be the toughest ever. It certainly made the headlines".

"Yes" she said, "that's just how this stupid lot carry on. Everyone will go out now and buy television sets, cameras and freezers before the Budget and defeat the whole object. It was the same when they brought the travel restrictions in; the silly devils announced in July that restrictions would start on the first of November and everyone then took out enough in August for the next two years. We did . We leave our spare funds with the barman at the hotel".

"My Lady" I said, stepping back about a yard, "I don't think you ought to say any more. I'm in the Bank of England".

"Oh, it's alright", she replied, "we've spent most of it since. We just send out the Cash Gift Allowances to him now and he saves them for our holiday".

The Cash Gift Allowances are gifts to non-residents, strictly for their own use. "My Lady" I said, "I'd rather not know, *please*".

At this juncture, Sir Charles joined us fresh from giving his instructions to the wine waiter. "Charles", said her Ladyship, "I've just been telling the Toastmaster about our account with Pedro ... " He smiled and was about to speak when I blurted out, "And I've been trying to tell your Lady, Sir, that I work in the Bank of England, Exchange Control – where I am in charge of the TRAVEL SECTION".

For a brief moment Sir Charles' Knighthood slipped and he joined the ranks of ordinary husbands as he looked at his wife. "Shut up you silly bitch", he murmured.

---

14. A freezing hot night in Brompton

Starting up a brand new hotel which offers all mod. cons. including Banqueting, can be an ulcer-making job. So much can go wrong. It's a bit like taking a new warship out on trials – except that with a warship you take only professional seamen and civilian experts. With a new hotel you have to let the public into the act. The dear British Public ...

I attended one of the first banquets at a new hotel in Brompton. It was to honour the retirement of a very popular headmaster from the Fulham and North Kensington Evening Institute and from the hotel's point of view it wasn't going too well.

The Head Waiter had hitherto been only a waiter (albeit a good one); the waitresses were mainly Nurses, relatively untrained in banqueting work, who wanted to make a pound or two; the 'orchestra' comprised three eighteen year olds from the Institute, specialising I think in violin, bassoon and flute work for funerals; the man in charge of the wines dispense bar was suddenly rushed to hospital with acute appendicitis; the air conditioning was on the blink – and so on.

The guests, who were extremely nice, jolly people did not seem aware of the crises 'below stairs'. True they got a little agitated about the non-arrival of their wines until the sweet course, and some mentioned gently that the room was getting warm (it was stifling) but no one actually got nasty until from the end of the Sprig "E" a rather haughty lady complained to me that she was freezing cold.

"Cold Madam?" I gasped. "You mean hot, don't you?"

"I know if I'm hot or cold, young man" she snapped, "there's a terrible draught on my shoulder and its bound to start my arthritis off again. You don't know what it's ..."

"Madam" I interrupted, "could I suggest that you change seats with Lord ... opposite? He's just been saying he's too hot". "I will not!" she hissed, fiercely. "Get the electrician at once and stop that damned draught!"

I fled. Women!

Finding the Head Waiter, I started to tell him about the fierce lady. It was another straw for his nearly broken back...

"Let the old cow wait" he said.

I didn't pursue the subject further. The poor chap was obviously nearing the end of his tether. Perhaps a little psychology would help.

"Mac" I said, confidentially, "I take my hat off to you. Your first night as Head Waiter, all these things going wrong for you and yet you've kept as cool as a cucumber. Marvellous. You'll make a great Head Waiter".

I could almost see the Death Wish leaving his body. "Really?" he beamed.

"Absolutely" I comforted him "you're doing marvellously".

The few words of comfort did him a world of good as they would do any of us. He actually laughed – but then he made a terrible mistake. "Everything's happened tonight, hasn't it?" he said. "I've had the lot in one go. Nothing worse could happen, could it?"

AT THAT VERY MOMENT, with a very loud clanking sound, a thirty foot long heavy curtain which stretched from floor to ceiling, started to move along the wall at the end of the sprigs.

"Oh! My God!" screamed Mac, all his new found confidence and joy leaving him, "What's happened now?"

What was happening was that one of the sound proofed curtains, used for dividing the great ballroom into smaller compartments, had started shuffling along very noisily towards the awful orchestra.

Nearing them it abruptly turned left and, amid screams of terror, and laughter, started coming up, parallel with the outside sprig, towards the top table. The musicians, mouths hanging open, gradually vanished from sight.

The Head Waiter must have known what would happen next for he screamed to waitresses near the magic curtain, "Stop it. Stop it!"

Too late. The curtain suddenly took <u>another</u> left hand turn and now the thirty foot monster, with a stout waitress clinging to its side laughing hysterically, bore down menacingly on the first sprig.

Thinking there might be some sort of panic I dashed for the microphone. The Headmaster beat me to it, thank goodness and made a more calming announcement than I could ever have dreamed up.

"Ladies and Gentlemen" he cried, "don't worry – they're only changing the bed pans!"

Guffaws of laughter from guests (and our nurse-waitresses) familiar with this hospital routine, mounting to an absolute roar as the curtain dragged over the table, separating man from wife, knives from forks and isolating about twenty people from the rest of us.

On went the curtain, seemingly an irresistible force, towards the next table. I'll never forget the face of one man, gulping his sweet down and constantly looking over his right shoulder as the thing bore down upon him. Over him it went, then over his table, with twenty further poor souls lost, before blessed relief, it stopped. No clanking, nothing. It was a bit like those war time days when the doodle-bugs' engines suddenly cut off ...

The show had to go on of course, and while coffee was being served (either side of the Iron Curtain) the electrician arrived. Quite an arrival too. About six foot four tall, eighteen stone, and hair down to his shoulders, he was suddenly framed in the doorway with a thirty foot ladder on his shoulder and a "WOT'S 'APPENED 'ERE?" expression on his face.

He couldn't get by the curtain to investigate the trouble and so had to be led round behind the Headmaster. Now that's an unusual sight; a long haired giant with an enormous ladder tramping the length of the top table (It wouldn't do for the Mansion House).

Ultimately, Tarzan reached the spot, at the end of sprig E, from whence the curtain had started its exciting journey. Placing the ladder against the wall there, and no doubt conscious that every eye was upon him, he sprang athletically on to it and started to run up. Unfortunately half way up he found the ladder was shaking so much under his great bulk and speed that he had to stop dead, hang on for dear life and then come down again – very slowly indeed.

He then, before I could stop him, approached the distinguished looking gentleman at the end of sprig 'E' who had earlier told me he was too hot.

"Ere mate" he panted, "'old the ladder for us, will ya?"

"Don't bother, MY LORD" I blurted, just in time, "I'll hold it".

The electrician then, amid cheers, mounted the ladder again and disappeared through an inspection trap in the ceiling. I waited patiently to see if he could persuade the electrically controlled curtain to retrace its steps but no such luck. He came down ponderously and looked very worried.

"Blimey mate" he breathed, "we've 'ad a lucky escape there. The 'lectric-moater's jumped right 'orf its tracks and if it 'adn't got caught in the wires that pulls those curtains back an forward, it would 'ave crashed dahn on those people. And it weighs two 'undredweight!"

"Is it safe now?" I enquired, nervously.

"Yus, the wire's still 'olding it an I've put an iron bar under it too".

"How the hell did it happen?"

"Well, some stoopid nit musta pushed one of these buttons 'ere (pointing to the wall) an started the curtains moving. Then 'e musta lost 'is 'ead and started pushing the other free buttons. It's caused murder up there – about free fousand quid's wortha damage".

"Strewth" I said, "but why should anyone press those four buttons?"

"Well … they might fink they was for the light or the 'eating".

The heating! I spun round to sprig E, to find the haughty lady looking very guilty indeed. Before I could speak, she said, defiantly, "Well I was so cold …".

"Madam" I said sternly "I think you should leave your name with the Manager".

"I will not!" she shouted.

I had no option but to take her place card from the table and later I gave it to the manager.

"That's the lady who caused three thousand pounds worth of damage to your new hotel, cut off about forty people from view and nearly caused a terrible accident" I said. "As long as you've got the name, you'll be able to find her …"

"Sully" he sighed "we won't even try. She was cold because of our system, the buttons shouldn't have been within public reach and there should never be any danger of two-hundred weight engines falling through the ceiling of a banqueting room. Any publicity would cripple us. Forget it".

So Haughty Lady, got away with it. Not a single word was ever said.

The Dear British Public.

———————

15. The old Tiffinian

———————

There are two very large and quite separate banqueting rooms at the Grosvenor House Hotel. The Great Hall – seating up to 1500 guests and the Ballroom which takes about 550.

Guests arriving at the hotel and possibly thinking that their Association's function is the only one being held there that evening, quite often stroll confidently to the Ballroom, give their names to the Toastmaster, are announced, received by the Chairman and given a drink before it dawns upon them that they are with the wrong collection of people. Some slink off and others come back to apologise to the Chairman – who invariably laughs away their embarrassed offers to pay for any drink consumed.

One Thursday evening this happened three times in the early stages of the reception so I started to ask each of the arriving guests, "Which function, Sir?" If they said, "The Oil Club" I directed them to the Great Hall. If they said, "The Golf Society" I said, "This way, Sir".

No more real trouble after that (except that the poor old Toastmaster had to say "Which function, Sir?" some four hundred times!) until towards the end of the reception period I observed a porter assisting a small and very ancient gentleman down the short flight of stairs towards me.

"Good evening Sir" I smiled, "which function, please?"

With shaking hand he passed an invitation card to me; I glanced at it quickly to see if it was headed "Oil Club" or "Golf Society". Neither – it said "Old Tiffinians".

"Have we got the 'Old Tiffinians' in one of the smaller rooms, Bert?" I asked the porter.

"Ole Tiffins?" "Nuffin like that, mate" said Bert – "gis a look at that card".

Taking it from my hand he examined it carefully … "It's the Dorchester" he cried, "you've got the wrong 'otel, Guv".

The old boy's face clouded and I'm sure mine did too. Poor old chap.

"Don't worry Sir" I comforted him, "the Dorchester's not too far away. Just turn left out of the door and it's about four hundred yards down".

" 'Old on, 'old on" interrupted Bert "It was for Wednesday night".

Wednesday night! That was the night before! Oh! What a terrible shame. Wrong function, wrong hotel and now wrong night. Even tomorrow night would have been bearable but last night – that was pathetic.

We explained the sad story to the Chairman, who had been watching patiently. Fortunately he had a heart big enough to insist that the Old Tiffinian come in and have one or two – or – more glasses of sherry with some friendly golfers.

So perhaps something of the old man's evening was saved. But poor chap – I can't think of anything worse, socially, than to dress up and come to town tonight for last night's Dinner.

---

16. Money is the root

Australian High Society is, to put it mildly, somewhat less respectful of protocol than its English counterpart. I should not, therefore, have been surprised, many years ago, to have experienced some slightly awkward moments as Toastmaster for an Australian bride's wedding reception at one of London's world famous hotels.

This bride was the thirty-three year old daughter of an Australian farmer who'd died earlier in the year of the wedding, leaving her three million pounds; her groom was a very distinguished English military man, some twenty years her senior and his nineteen year old son by a previous marriage was Best Man. Not one of those "Love's young dream" marriages by a long chalk, but everyone seemed very, very happy – especially the Mother of the Bride, who'd been left <u>six</u> million pounds by her husband and who, to this casual observer, seemed to be making the best of it.

Noticing that guests were beginning to arrive and gather in the foyer, I interrupted the Family party (Bride, Groom, Best Man, Parents and two very handsome young Latin types) during their third bottle of champagne, to request, politely, that they form up to start receiving.

"Certainly" called Mother, in her strong Australian accent, "How do we line up?"

"Well … you first Madam, as our Hostess, then normally the Father of the Bride, as Host, but in the circumstances perhaps a son or brother, then the parents of the Groom, then the Bride and lastly the Groom".

"It can't be me husband" she chortled, "the poor old womba's just kicked the bucket. It'll have to be me boy friend". And, turning to the taller of the two handsome Latinos, she called "Alfredo! Come and stand here!" – indicating that he should stand <u>first</u> in line.

Protocol-wise this was so wrong (Alfredo was if anything younger than the Bride (let alone the Hostess) was not related and spoke very little English), that even the patient and tolerant Toastmaster started to twitch and feel that he should render a gentle rebuke.

Someone behind him put paid to this notion, however, with a soft tap on his shoulder and a warning glance. It was the wise, dignified old Head Waiter – watching everything.

So the reception proceeded, with Alfredo making a complete hash of everything, including kissing all the male guests as they were announced, Mother and the Bride getting more and more noisy and the rather genteel English Groom and his parents turning pinker and pinker.

A further high point in the proceedings was reached when Mother, exclaiming "Me trotters are killing me!" took off her rather large shoes and placed them in front of her.

I glanced despairingly toward the Head Waiter, silently seeking support for some action such as pushing the shoes to the rear of the line, but again received that almost imperceptible warning glance.

The final blow came as I announced "The Right Honourable the Lord and the Lady …".

"Hello, you old bastards" roared Mother, "why weren't you at the church?"

This was too much, and while both Alfredo and Mother were kissing his Lordship all over, I turned desperately to the Head Waiter and hissed, "Can't I calm her down a bit? She's doing everything wrong!"

"Son" he replied, and I've always remembered his wisdom, "Listen. In this hotel, if she's got six million pounds, <u>everything she does is right</u>".

17. The gate crashers

Gatecrashers at cocktail parties can be quite a problem. They are not your normal hooligans and yobs, who are ill at ease in great hotels, but intelligent, suave, steely-nerved persons who cannot resist the urge to obtain free drinks in charming company.

In their appearance, manner and bearing they are indistinguishable from the invited guests; and sometimes they have perfectly-forged invitation cards too! Which doesn't give a Toastmaster much of a chance, really.

We do have our successes, however, like the time when, at a reception for the opening of a new Branch of the Tokai Bank, I was announcing the names and organisations of the guests on arrival so that the English Manager (ex-Bank of England) could pass them on to his visiting Japanese chairman. In the main the four hundred guests were from the other London Banks, or from the Tokai Bank's own customers (London branches of Japanese companies). The manager knew some by sight and others he'd often talked to by 'phone, but the rest were complete strangers to him. Thus the Toastmaster's 'name and job' announcements were very useful as reminders or introductions.

I announced one arrival, a fine-looking, horn-rimmed executive type as, 'Mr Ward of the B.B.C.' After shaking hands warmly with the Manager and the Chairman, 'Mr Ward' graciously accepted a whisky from a tray offered by a waiter and passed into the hall to join the happy throng.

Guests were arriving in a long stream, but when there was a lull, some ten minutes or so later, the Manager called, "Good to get the B.B.C. here eh, Ben?"

"Yes" I agreed. "Have you got a contact there, Sir?"

"No" he said, slightly excited, "but they've probably heard about the opening; a bit of publicity won't hurt us …"

I nodded agreement, but I must say a little seed of doubt had been sown.

Shortly after this the Head Waiter came over to check from my hand tally-counter whether most of the guests had arrived. (He wanted to judge whether it was time to serve the hot food).

After I'd told him the number I'd clicked in, he stayed with me for a while. "You know that bloke you announced as Mr Ward of the B.B.C?" he murmured.

"Yes?" I answered quickly.

"Well … Last night he was Mr Barnes of Reuters".

"Honestly?"

"I'm telling you". "And last week he was Mr Wilson of the Daily Telegraph".

That did it! We'd all been polite, servile and (the hosts) generous to Mr Ward and he was nothing but a regular crook.

I suddenly found myself in the centre of the room, banging the gavel for silence. "Gentlemen", I called, "I'm sorry to interrupt but we have an urgent message for a Mr Ward of the B.B.C. Is he present, please?"

He was. Tucked in at a small table behind a very large whisky, with two of the most respectable bankers you've ever seen and, like everybody else, looking calmly and innocently round to see where the B.B.C. man was.

The cool cheek … But the Head Waiter was watching and I wasn't going to be beaten. "Ah! *There* you are Sir," I said, walking up to our shyster. "I'm glad I've found you; would you kindly have a quick word with your Secretary, outside. This way Sir".

He *had* to come. Nodding pleasantly to the two bankers he followed me outside, where the Head Waiter was standing with a doorman, about seven feet high and not quite as broad.

"Mr Ward of the B.B.C., Sir?" asked the Head Waiter politely.

"Er, yes".

"SHOVE OFF", said the Head Waiter (or something to that effect).

Mr Ward Shoved off.

"Goodnight, Mr Barnes of Reuters," jeered the foyer attendant.

"Goodnight, Mr Wilson of the Daily Telegraph," called the doorman.

I don't suppose "Mr Ward" will ever come back to that hotel again, even as a genuine guest. I wonder where he operates now.

18. Love from above

The fascination of Toastmastering, for me at least, is that one deals with all sorts of people who do all sorts of things. Take a wedding reception at the Arts Club ...

It was all very nice. A lovely Bride and a handsome Groom received the happy guests on a magnificent balcony at the top of a gracious, curved stairway and from the balcony the guests passed into a typical clubroom. The usual deep armchairs, some tables with magazines like the Tatler spread about and a few large china bowls absolutely full of rose petals (I'm told they're called Pot-Pourri). Also, more importantly for the guests, a modern bar, which on this occasion was serving champagne as though from a fountain.

After they'd had an hour and a half at this pleasant and civilised pastime, the guests were requested to follow the Bride and Bridegroom down to the Drawing Room on the ground floor.

Glasses of champagne in hand they good naturedly trooped down the great stairway and gathered in the Drawing Room in front of the wedding cake.

The happy couple then cut the cake, amid a lot of cheerful banter and, after the Host, the Groom and the Best Man had all made very humorous and kindly speeches, the Bride and Bridegroom 'mingled' for about twenty minutes. Then it was time for them to go.

The Best Man went to get the car and I asked the guests 'to line the sides and also assemble outside the Club – ready to give your Bride and Bridegroom a really good send off!' (This was mainly so that the caterer could close the bar for the sake of our host's pocket!)

Whilst the guests were taking up their positions I checked with the young couple that they had their passports, that their bags were in the car and so on.

Then, after placing the bride on the groom's left arm and a bottle of champagne in his right hand (he wouldn't be parted from the glass of champagne in his left hand), I led them forward into the crowd which had chosen to assemble in the well of the stairway with the time honoured shout of 'Here they come'.

As we slowly pushed through amid the joyous cries and the well wishes, there came a tremendous crash of broken glass. I spun quickly, expecting to see that the Groom had dropped his precious bottle of champagne. Instead I saw a lady staggering toward me with blood streaming from her forehead!

Something inside told me that no bride would wish to see such a sight on her wedding day so I passed the injured lady to a chap on my left with the urgent request 'Look after this lady's head, please Sir' grabbed the Bride and Groom and pulled them through to the street where the remainder of the guests, unaware that anything was wrong, were cheering like mad.

"What was that crash?" asked the Bride, as covered in confetti, she climbed into the car.

"I don't know Madam", I lied, "but as long as it wasn't your bottle of champagne, everything's alright". And to the hearty cheers and shouts of "Be Good!" they went off to what I hope was an exciting honeymoon.

Dashing back to the numbed crowd of guests in the well of the stairway, I was appalled to see the floor covered in rose petals, large pieces of china and... Blood! A terrible sight at a wedding.

What had happened was that one of the more romantic of the male guests had had what he thought was the nice idea of raining rose petals down on the Bride from the high balcony. Had dashed up the stairs grabbed a pot-pourri bowl and man-like, tipped it over as the Bride and Bridegroom passed through the crowd below him.

There should have been a nice great cloud of rose petals like the Royal Albert Hall on Remembrance Night; instead the petals AND THE THICK CHINA INNER LINING of the pot-pourri bowl had come down like a bomb on the head of a girl who was just about to kiss the Bride!

How nasty for the girl with the gashed forehead!

How terrible for the romantic petal thrower!

How lucky for the Bride! The bowl lining missed her by about nine inches!

---

19. An evening at the Elephant

Appointed as the Master of Ceremonies for the Junior Lightweight Championship of the World between Brian Mitchell of South Africa and Jim McDonnel of London at the Leisure Centre, Elephant and Castle, on the 2nd November 1988, I found, as the great day neared, that politics threatened to rob me of a night's pay – and my fourteenth World Championship.

Firstly, Southwark Council, having months before signed an agreement with the promoter, Mickey Duff, got cold feet over the fact that the defending champion was a white South African, and cancelled the booking of the Centre. Then Mickey got tough threatening to sue the Council for all the considerable expenses he had incurred, based upon their written agreement – and they promptly gave in. The Big Fight (and my fee) was on again.

Or was it? On the very day of the Tournament, the Council workers' union withdrew their co-operation. Thus there would be no door staff, no electricians, no security, no seat arrangers etc. on duty.

The indefatigable Mickey got over this by bringing in some of his own staff. Not enough to do the job perfectly – for instance they didn't have time to letter the rows and number the seats – but sufficient to prepare the Centre for a night of boxing.

I was always given a free ticket for my wife Rosie, so this night, after parking the car in one of the gloomy, under-the-arches, litter strewn, narrow streets at the Elephant (would it be there when we returned?) and then walking through the ominous, foreboding graffiti-covered underpass, she and I arrived at the darkened Leisure Centre.

There was a considerable police presence but no visible sign of an entrance.

Having wandered round the building in an unsuccessful search for an open door, I decided (as I'd done on previous occasions) to "bunk in" where the great B.B.C. Television van was stationed. I knew from past experience that there would be an opening there to allow passage of the thick cables from van to ringside.

A policeman inside (probably forced to work on his night off) very firmly turned us away, however, but then was kind enough to point out the only official, strictly controlled entrance for the evening.

To get to it we had to pass through a sea of some two hundred swaying, chanting, black, anti-apartheid protestors; a bit worrying, but it had to be done.

"Rosie", I enquired, "what's that they're chanting?" "Mitchell OUT", "Mitchell OUT" she replied.

"Right! Start chanting "I grunted and, ever the gentleman, let her go through first, with both of us chanting, "Mitchell OUT", "Mitchell OUT".

I'd had the sense to put on my old gor-blimey cloth cap and to cover my black bow tie with a dirty blue scarf, so the crowd, for a while, possibly thought that we were white sympathisers but, as we neared the guarded door, they changed their chant to "Shame on YOU!" "Shame on YOU!" in which we declined to join.

After a small altercation with the policeman guarding the door (who refused to believe that the scruffy chap in front of him was the M.C., until shown the black tie and Board of Control Licence) we were in, to a chorus of boos from our fellow chanters.

Then it was on to my normal pre-fight routine. Checking the boxers' names, weights and order of appearance; the referee and timekeeper for each contest; the names of celebrities who should be introduced into the ring prior to the Main Event, and the B.B.C's special requirements.

All was satisfactory until I came to the checking of the microphones. To my horror these had been sabotaged by the council workers! I would have to use lung-power alone to make myself heard over the considerable noise of some 1200 boxing fans! And the Main Event was coming on last – by which time I would have no voice left for my televised announcement! Nor for my Toastmastering engagements during the rest of the week!

When the boxers came into the ring for the first contest, I decided to appeal to the crowd to help me; but this very appeal was going to be extremely difficult to put over as, apart from the usual good natured hubbub there were fierce arguments going on by the ringside between the posh people who'd paid £75 for a numbered seat only to find no seat was numbered or row lettered!

Asking the Timekeeper to attract attention by a very long ring on his bell, I bellowed "Ladies and Gentlemen, as you can see, the mike has gone for a Burton. Would you kindly help me during the evening, and whenever you hear the bell rung like this ("Ting-a-ling-a-ling-a-ling" went the Timekeeper again) please give me your RAPT attention".

They sportingly listened to me in silence and my spirits rose accordingly; but then some sailor at the back roared, something like "ROLLOCKS". (Collapse of stout M.C.!).

There being no alternative, I pressed on, regardless of the effect such howling against the mob would have on my precious Toastmaster's vocal chords, and announced the first three contests.

By then, however, I was attracting some good natured comments like "Eh? Eh? Can't 'ear yer!" and was getting seriously worried whether I'd last out until the Main Event – in front of millions of viewers!

Suddenly, a brilliant thought hit me! I'd seen a police inspector outside, controlling the protesting crowds with a "bull horn". Could I perhaps borrow it?

Signalling a young constable to come to the ringside (which caused a ripple of worry in the audience) I asked him if he could pop out, explain my situation to the Inspector and see if he would lend me this voice-saving piece of equipment.

It worked! The young copper came back proudly with it (plus a few threats about what would happen to me if I damaged or lost it) and I was saved.

Until the Main Event that is, because the B.B.C. then insisted that they didn't want me to use the bull horn for a televised big fight announcement.

So we compromised and, amid the tremendous noise which accompanies every Main Event introduction, I made my announcement close by the ropes on the B.B.C. Camera side of the ring and they held their microphones as near to me as they could without getting them into the picture.

It worked beautifully, apparently, and the viewers heard every word; which is more than could be said for the poor punters who paid £75 for the unnumbered, misplaced seats ("Oh! Sod them" said the B.B.C. technician).

Quite a memorable night out – and the car was still there when we got back!.

20. Jennifer (and the Queen) really fixed it

One day in 1982 a beautiful young girl of about fourteen, from the Liverpool area, asked "Jim to Fix it" so that she could perform as Toastmaster at a Big Banquet.

Jimmy Savile's team accepted the challenge and asked the Guildhall London, if it could be arranged.

Shortly afterwards I was asked to train the young lady sufficiently enough for her to make a couple of announcements during the Association of Chief Constables' Annual Luncheon at Guildhall.

She proved an apt pupil and a very attractive personality and the show was quickly, and successfully, "in the can".

The next big step was the actual appearance on the T.V. show "Jim'll Fix It" at which the video went over very well indeed.

Before we parted, both families had become good friends, exchanged addresses holiday maker style and I promised that, whenever young Jennifer decided to marry, I would be her Toastmaster, free, as a wedding present.

Eight years later, after regularly exchanging Christmas cards with us, her Mother secretly revealed that Jennifer was to marry in Liverpool on the 16th June 1990. I therefore just as secretly arranged to be there to greet her at the Reception as she stepped down from the Bridal Carriage. It was lovely! She being completely surprised.

Something more, too. Because that sunny happy day, the day that Jennifer had chosen to marry, was the very day that her two principal fellow actors on the show appeared in the Queen's Birthday Honours – Jimmy with a knighthood, me with an M.B.E!

Life can be very strange!

21. Old skinny legs

Under various Incentive Schemes in the U.S.A., top salesmen and their families are rewarded with four day trips to swinging London.

Soon after their arrival, at places like the Hilton, Grosvenor House and the Royal Garden Hotels, they attend a cocktail party or dinner and meet some of Britain's Olde Worlde characters; Town Criers, Guardsmen, Toastmasters, Trumpeters, Pearly Kings and so on, which corny as these may appear to the locals, the Americans lap up.

I was once asked to act as Town Crier to greet the top sellers of Lincoln Cars on their arrival at the Hilton. I'd always fancied the old 'Oyez, Oyez' performance, so I accepted with alacrity.

First thing of course was to obtain a Town Crier's outfit, and this meant a visit to Monty Berman's theatrical costume vault in darkest Kensington. (There's an interesting place; about the size of three bank vaults, absolutely filled with clothes to equip everyone from a tribe of Ancient Britons, through Cavaliers and Cowboys to astronauts).

When I asked for a Town Crier's outfit, the Manager looked at me, mumbled to himself "Short, portly", walked away and returned within minutes with some perfectly fitting regalia, including size 8½ buckled shoes!

On trying the outfit on again at home, for the cruel amusement of the family, I found that the grey half-stockings, which were attached to the knee-breeches, kept wrinkling. This clearly was not good enough for top Lincoln salesmen and my clever wife came with an efficient but uncomfortable solution – my daughter's white tights!

With a mace borrowed from a team of dancing girls, I was now ready to meet any Lincoln, Ford (or at a pinch even Leyland) salesman.

Came the great night and the salesmen and their families were sipping cocktails in the ballroom. I waited behind a screen in buckled shoes, too tight white tights, doe-skin breeches, red and gold embroidered frocked coat, lace jabot, frilly cuffs, and tri-cornered black and gold hat. I looked gorgeous!

On a signal, I rang the hotel's fire bell several times and bellowing "Oyez – Oyez", strode in among the startled visitors.

Stopping in the centre I dramatically opened a scroll and proclaimed, "Oyez – Oyez – Oyez! All ye good people gathered here in the cause of pleasure, draw near and give your attention!" (Tri-cornered hat swung into the air) "God save the Queen! God ..." (a little hesitation at this point; I was going to say "God save the President" but Watergate was in the news, so I finished "...save America!") I am commanded by the Right Honourable the Lord Mayor of London to welcome you to this fair city and to express the hope that you will enjoy every moment of your holiday here".

Hat lifted again.

"God – save – the – Queen".

A courtly bow to the poor old tourists and I was away, amid rapturous applause, to collect the quickest fee I'd ever earned.

It's a good feeling, the applause, the money ... "Sullivan, you old ham", I said to myself as I neared the door, "this is better than banking".

But bankers wouldn't have been so unkind as the waiters at the door, who, as I passed majestically by, yelled, "OLD SKINNY LEGS!"

22. Go seawards young man

Early in 1940 I joined a train in London en route to Skegness for my first day in the Navy.

I found myself with perhaps eighty other excited young men bound for the Navy or the Army; all very much of a pattern, similarly dressed in the fashion of the day but from all sorts of backgrounds. A nice lot of chaps, though, and I remember quietly wondering who were for the Navy and who for the Army; who would maybe become war-heroes; who would be crippled, blinded, drowned, killed – or come through unscathed. I still sometimes wonder about this…

The journey passed quickly and Skegness Station soon came into view. We became noticeably quieter. "What happens now?" was the question in our minds. It was quite a moment in our young lives…

For the Army recruits the answer came almost immediately. A frighteningly upright, smart and tough-looking sergeant suddenly appeared and roared, "All men for the Army! Outside with your bags and form up in the road – NOW!"

The embryo soldiers, strangely quiet and worried, obeyed with alacrity. Within seconds, it seemed, they were out on the road and being subjected to a series of barked instructions and commands culminating in a, "Right Turn! Quick March!" Which saw some sixty bewildered, out-of-step young lads moving off to their new life.

They left behind, now on the platform, some twenty equally worried (but better looking) budding sailors – pretty shaken at what they'd just witnessed.

Not for long though. Two Navy trucks drew up and from the second an elderly, kindly Chief Petty Officer emerged and ambled towards us, smiling broadly.

"You lads for the Navy?" He called.

"Yes Sir" we chorused.

"Don't call me Sir" he said, "I'm only a Chief – 'Ere who wants their first Navy tickler?" handing round some duty-free cigarettes.

As we breathed a sigh of relief and the smokers lit up, he continued, "Put your cases in that first truck lads, and then climb aboard the second one. I'll be with you in a minute."

True to his word he was back in time to assist the last couple of his new shipmates climb on to the open truck and check that we were all seated comfortably. Then, with a cheery, "Away we go lads to our first ship, the stone frigate (i.e. Naval Shore Establishment) H.M.S. Royal Arthur." he joined the driver.

So off we went, feeling a lot better. About a mile up the road we passed a party of men, dressed in civilian clothes, each carrying a suitcase in his left hand, being bullied along by a very upright Sergeant, snapping out orders like, "Heads Up" or "Left, Right", Left, Right."

To me that's always been the difference between the Army and the Navy. They in the road, we on the truck.

Anyway, we gave them a few ironic cheers as we sailed past and one of our number made the very percipient observation "Poor sods!"

When, minutes later, we arrived at H.M.S. Royal Arthur (the former Butlin's Holiday Camp), the first thing we saw, in great letters, high up on the wall, was Butlin's motto:-

"Our true intent is all for your delight".

Now the Army would have had <u>that</u> down – quick!

23. The ensemble

Dining at my small table behind the top table one night at Grosvenor House, I became pleasantly aware that the orchestra was playing one selection after another of the beautiful Viennese melodies which I love. A glance at the back of the menu seemed to provide the answer. It said 'Dinner music by Josef Butel'. That explained it – Viennese music by Viennese musicians.

For an hour I enjoyed it all, beautiful music, soft lights, gorgeous food and wine and superb service. (What a pity my wife was at home doing the ironing!).

Guests, happily wining, dining and chatting to old friends are often either unaware of the music or too shy to start a round of applause for it. This is rather sad because the banquet musicians are not only craftsmen who do a good job but also artistes who enjoy 'taking a bow' during or after a performance.

On this evening in particular, I thought the audience had been given very good value but had shown little response. At the coffee stage I therefore announced, 'My Lords, Ladies and Gentlemen may I ask you please to show your appreciation for the lovely music during dinner from (in my best European) Yosef Bootel and the Ensomb'.

This brought forth a fine burst of clapping and cheers and the leader (who I thought looked like Johanne Strauss) waved to me in thanks. He made as if to come round to me but as I had just been told by the Chairman to start the speeches as soon as possible I signalled him, in a friendly manner, not to bother. With the other musicians he then went home.

The next day I received a message on our telephone answering machine, in ripe Cockney, 'Joe Buttle 'ere. Jes rang to say fanks from me an the boys for the bild-up larce nigh'.

24. The shy chef

For a chap with an Irish name, I've a surprisingly high opinion of the English. I happen to think they are the most inventive, just, tolerant and civilised race on earth. They don't make a great show of patriotism but I'm sure that, well hidden in their souls, they have a fierce love of their great country and all it stands for.

Some of this is revealed to me each year when I do the St. George's Day Banquet of the Royal Society of St. George. The main speech is always a really moving one and it culminates in what for me is the most thrilling toast of the year – ENGLAND! (Not a dry eye in the house!).

The main course is naturally Roast Beef and on such a day, we honour the national dish. Sirloin is carried in by the Chef (a quiet, shy back-room boy) and he is escorted by a drum party from one of the Guards Regiments. Thereby, of course, hangs a tale – of a St. George's Night with a typical English chairman and a typical English chef.

The fish course had been cleared and, after a discreet exchange of signals between the Head Waiter, the electrician and myself, I announced, "Mr Chairman, My Lords, Ladies and Gentlemen, be pleased to welcome the Roast Beef of England!" The lights suddenly dimmed and from a doorway in the left-hand corner of the hall came the sound of drums. A searchlight stabbed on, picking out four giant Guardsmen, two leading, two following, a rather small chef, who carried a silver tray of sirloin. "Burroomp ti bomp, burroomp ti boomp", went the drums and the Roast Beef party, amid great applause, proceeded from left to right along the front of the Top Table.

Approaching the centre, where the Chairman now stood waiting to receive them, the sergeant bawled, "Partee – Halt". The Party halted. "Ry-eet – Turn". The Party turned right and were now facing the Chairman, the Guardsmen tall, upright and immaculate (except that one now had a little beef gravy on his tunic) the Chef small and, I thought, rather miserable; but so far, so good.

Now it was the Chairman's turn. Reading from a small index card (I wish they'd learn their spiel) he gave the Traditional Address. "Chef!" he cried, "I charge you to declare that this beef is fit for the consumption and delight of my Guests".

"Do you so declare?"

The Chef, who I suspect couldn't tell St. George from St. Cohen, and would have much preferred to have been left in his kitchen, said, "YUS, Mate".

For a moment it seemed the Sergeant's bearskin would blow off! Military discipline prevailed however. "Right turn!!" he screamed, "Quick march".

Burroomp ti bomp – burroomp ti boomp – back to the kitchen, where the Chef, restored to his own element cut the beef superbly.

Some blossom only in the shade; others only in the sunlight.

Presumably that's why some become Chefs and some Toastmasters?

---

25. A great honour

This may surprise some of my readers but I started the Toastmastering more to meet great and interesting people than to make money.

The person I most wanted to meet, talk to, or even just look at, was my hero Sir Winston Churchill. I had to wait a long time to fulfil this ambition… perhaps too long.

I was officiating at a small but very select cocktail party for Governors General of the Colonies in one of the small rooms at the Savoy. I'd announced these gentlemen at the door (all twenty five of them – I reckon I was getting about 20p a word) and had nothing further to do but stand there for about an hour – mainly, I imagine, to discourage would-be gatecrashers.

Very many famous people passed along the busy corridor, a surprising number of whom I knew by name or by sight. Many stopped for a chat, and time passed very pleasantly indeed until from inside the room I sensed and heard the unmistakable signs of the impending departure of some of my guests.

"ORFLI glad you asked me old boy," "Terribli kind of you to come", "Veri nice parti" and so on.

Just at that moment, however, the hotel detective approached at a brisk pace. "Sully" he said, "lock that door".

"Lock the door?" I choked. "Lock the door?"

"Lock it!" he ordered.

I locked it.

"What on earth ...?" I started, with visions of some gang of assassins coming to kidnap all my Governors ...

"We're bringing Churchill along" he said, simply.

Churchill! In this narrow passage he must pass within two feet of me. Our Winnie – the man who saved us: the greatest Englishman. I stood there, thrilled as a schoolboy waiting to meet the Heavyweight champion of the world. The unfortunate Governors, now knocking on the door and calling "Open this do-ah!" could have been in another world for all I knew...

Suddenly, the Great Man was in sight ... Alas it was not the figure I knew so well. They were wheeling a tiny, wizened, man towards me; his mouth was drooping open, his skin was like alabaster; his

hands lay weakly on his knees. "Oh Winnie" I thought, "I'd forgotten <u>even you</u> had to get old." It was terribly sad.

"Sully" the detective interrupted my thoughts, "... Would you help me carry Sir Winston down the stairs?" (There were five steps just on my left).

Would I help carry Sir Winston Churchill?

"Of course" I said almost fiercely, and swelling with pride helped to pick up the great man and carry him down the steps. I was within inches of his ear and couldn't resist whispering into it, "God bless you, Sir".

That's a moment I'll never forget.

I carried Winston Churchill.

26. Oh! What a surprise

The Royal College of Surgeons in England and Wales is situated at Lincoln's Inn Fields. It is of course a great seat of learning and the meeting place of some of the greatest surgeons in the world.

From my, perhaps rather simple, viewpoint they are great men; brilliantly clever, decisive, down to earth, approachable, cultured – they seem to have everything. Then it emerges that they were Olympic athletes in their youth and won a couple of awards for gallantry during the war. They also give very fine, witty and learned speeches at their banquets.

The Privy Council is another body for which we must of course have a similar admiration.

It consists of eminent persons able to act "with others" upon the demise of the Sovereign, or able to advise the Sovereign on many matters of State.

The Clerk of the Council is Sir Godfrey Agnew, K.C.V.O. who, in my book must have one of the most responsible and dignified jobs in Britain. He is after all accountable for the day-to-day administration of a Council of which every member ranks higher in the List of Precedence than the Chancellor of the Exchequer and the Lord Chief Justice of England.

The appearance of such a high dignitary to respond for the other highly ranked guests, after a really top-drawer Banquet at the prestigious Royal College of Surgeons, promised to be a meeting of the sublime and the exalted. I was therefore proud to introduce him thus, "Mr. President, Your Excellencies, Your Graces, My Lord Bishops, My Lords Ladies and Gentlemen, pray silence for the Response by The Clerk of Her Majesty's Most Honourable Privy Council, Sir Godfrey Agnew, Knight Commander of the Royal Victorian Order."

He stood up, immaculate and dignified with Orders and medals glistening and to our utter delight and astonishment rattled off, Max Miller style, at least thirty very good jokes.

27. If you can walk with kings

Guests of Honour at the Chamber of Shipping's Banquets, at Grosvenor House, always tended to be Prime Ministers, Ministers of State and the like. Of late however they have taken to inviting the royal sailors like Prince Philip and King Olav of Norway.

The day after I had looked after the Dinner for King Olav (and 1400 lesser mortals) I was engaged by the then Lord Mayor to officiate at his rather lush "Help the Aged Luncheon" at the Royal Garden Hotel, Kensington, when the hosts at each of the forty tables were to be famous and lively octogenarians. People like Jack Hulbert, Cicily Courtnedge and Jack Warrren who, by their example could show us how to lead very full lives, seemingly for ever.

I took the day off and made my way casually towards Kensington. I chose to go by Underground to Notting Hill, instead of taking a bus to Kensington High Street, and at Notting Hill chose to walk through Kensington Palace Gardens rather than bussing down to Kensington Church Street.

I was a lovely day, so I dawdled through the "Gardens" (sometimes known as Millionaires' Row) having a yarn with the resident security Beadles about an anti-Soviet demo then taking place at the end of the road, sympathising with a road sweeper who was trying to clear a half mile carpet of leaves which had fallen from the great plane trees and generally wasting time.

The various choices of route and casual stops, served to have me meandering past the IN and OUT drives of one particular Residence (No. 10) at one particular time.

Whilst doing so, I heard soft voices exchanging farewells, a bit of heel clicking and the precise closing of a limousine's doors.

A Rolls purred towards the exit and nosey-like, I stopped to let it go by so that I could see who was in it.

The chap beside the driver (a Scotland Yard man) and I recognised each other simultaneously but as I went to wave to him he turned to speak to the man in the back. Too late however, for as the car drew alongside, the electrically operated window was already humming down and the man in the back was leaning out with a lovely big smile …

"Good morning, Mr. Sullivan" said the King of Norway.

Sometimes I wonder how I keep my (very) common touch.

---

28. Fate

Slowly leaving a small roundabout, near Leatherhead, on my way to a wedding reception for the famous insurance family of Bowring, I noted that the minor road ahead was completely clear except for one car parked on the other side.

Just as I started to accelerate away I saw with horror the face of a white poodle dog nearly level with mine about two feet in front of my bonnet.

Slamming on the brakes I was apparently lucky enough to check the car sufficiently to allow the dog to drop to the ground in time to let the front go over without harm. My relief was short-lived, however, because there was a dull thud from somewhere under the back seats …

Jumping out and running to the back of the car, I found the little chap lying under the rear bumper. Picking him up gently, I was horrified to see blood start spurting from his mouth, over his beautiful white coat.

I laid him down by the curb stroking him and speaking to him in a low voice, "Steady boy. Steady boy" or something like that.

I could feel his heart beating tremendously fast but then suddenly, shockingly, it stopped.

"Oh God!" I said dully to the small crowd which had gathered "He's dead!"

"Poor little thing" said a woman, "he's been running among the traffic like a lost soul. We chased him away a couple of times."

"Thank Gawd he's dead before he caused a terrible accident" said the butcher.

"He caught his head on your crown wheel" said another chap. "I was following behind and saw it. Those poodles have got very brittle heads, you know."

"You'll have to report it – being a dog" he added.

The butcher came up with a cardboard box. I remember it had "Fray Bentos" printed on the side. "Put 'im in there chum. You'll have to take 'im to the coppers; the Station's about a mile up on the left."

Sadly I did as I was bid putting the box and its pathetic contents into the boot of the car.

At the police station the sergeant took all particulars of the accident. Calm and efficient he didn't seem as upset as I thought he should be.

"What do I do with the box?" I enquired, hesitant to mention what lay silently in it and half-hoping he'd say "Leave it here."

"Take it to the animal cemetery, Sir" he said. "First turning on the right, and about a mile up the hill you'll see a big gate on the left. Tell the blokes there I sent you."

The "animal cemetery" turned out to be the local sewerage farm. The chaps there were kind enough to me and even curious about my winged collar and white bow tie. "Leave it there mate" they said. "We'll look after it."

So I left it there – and went off to the wedding reception. I didn't feel very happy; I'd killed a nice dog and, in effect, had dumped him at a sewerage farm.

The reception went off well but my thoughts kept straying. Where had the little dog suddenly come from? And why had he jumped up so high in front of my car.

I thought about him all the way home and many, many times during the rest of the weekend.

On Monday a very nice letter arrived from the owner. He said he'd heard from the policeman that I'd seemed really cut up and that I shouldn't blame myself.

It was such a nice letter that I rang the man. He said, "I felt I should write because that same afternoon while I was giving my son a driving lesson a dog ran into the road in front of us. The boy swerved to avoid it and if I hadn't grabbed the wheel, we would have killed a family in a car coming the opposite way. I gave him a terrible blast and told him "if that happens again GO OVER THE DOG." Then when I got home I found my dog had been running in the road and had been killed."

"I honestly didn't see him at all until he appeared in the air in front of the car" I mused. "It almost seemed as though he'd jumped up to try to see me ..."

"Wait a minute" he interrupted. "What sort of car have you got?"

"It's a 1956 Ford Consul" I replied. "Why?"

"That's it" he exclaimed. "My daughter has a 1956 Consul and she takes him for a drive in it every Saturday. Last Saturday she took delivery of a new car and because she wanted to concentrate on the new controls she left him at home. I was out with the boy and we left the dog in the garden. He scraped away a big space under the front gate – you wouldn't believe it unless you saw it – and got out, searching and searching for his mistress's car. Then you came along."

A great weight was beginning to lift from my mind ...

"Mr. Sullivan" continued the kind voice – "What colour is your car?"

"Carlisle Blue" I said.

"Carlisle Blue? My God. It's exactly the same colour too. The same colour. It was fate."

And so it was. What else but fate could lead my Carlisle Blue Consul from Petts Wood to Leatherhead on the very day that girl decided to try out her new car.

Thank God I made that 'phone call.

29. Let them have anything they want

Called upon to officiate at a Nigerian wedding reception recently at a top London hotel, I was a bit disappointed on arrival to find that everything had been put back an hour and a half because of all things, the GROOM had arrived very, very late at the Church.

When, two hours later, the guests arrived, I announced them with their very strange names like "Mr Nbongsuwrey and Miss Abadonguta" to the Bride and Bridegroom. I'd been told to expect 150 guests and was very surprised to find, when my hand tally-counter showed a mere 60, that the queue was finished.

"Never mind" said the Bridegroom who seemed to be the organiser "we'll go into dinner without them".

"Now, Sir – without the other 90 guests?"

"Yes" he said.

It was all a bit strange, but I checked with the Head Waiter that all was ready.

"Ready for the larce two soddin 'ours" he growled. "Jus give us a chance ter ligh the candools…"

Back I went to the Bridegroom saying "I'm calling them in now Sir, would you and your Bride please wait behind? I'll take you two in separately".

"No. Wait a minute man – we'll go in at half past seven".

"That's another half an hour, Sir" I gasped.

"Yes …well … I've changed my mind" he smiled. He was a big, laughing, smiling boy, but a little mixed up, I began to suspect.

Back I went to the Banqueting Room and the suffering Head Waiter. "Sorry old son, he wants to leave it for half an hour".

"Blow the bleen't candools aht" he moaned to the waiters.

I slowly wended my way back along the corridor which separated the Banqueting Room from the Reception Hall only to be met, half-way, by Smiler the menace and about half the guests.

"We're coming in now, man "he chuckled.

I sprinted back to the Head Waiter, who seeing my face, said "Yeah! I know. They're comin in nah! LIGH THE CANDOOLS"

Then the laughing fuzzy haired mass was upon us and we guided them to the centre tables (so as to make the place look crowded) leaving the outside ones empty for possible late arrivals.

At Smiler's request I said Grace for them, using one of my "funnies". "For Boiled and Baked and Grilled and Roast, thank Father, Son and Holy Ghost," which gave them an hysterical fit of the giggles for some reason, then on came the food. Marvellous expensive food, fit for a King or an African Princess.

Walking back to my table (the Head Waiter had put the Disc jockey and me on one of the empty guest tables) I noticed three chauffeurs, who had been in at the Reception, wandering about looking lost.

"Are you alright lads?" I enquired, thinking they must be the Bridal Party's personal chauffeurs, "would you like to eat? There's gonna be about ninety spare dinners".

"We'd like to eat, chum" said the eldest chap "we've 'ad nuffink all day – but you'd better clear it wiv 'im" indicating the Bridegroom.

So, being a decent fellow I asked the Bridegroom if it would be alright for the three chauffeurs to have a meal with the Disc Jockey and myself. "It will help fill up another table, Sir…"

He was benevolence itself. "Let them have anything they want" he said grandly.

Thus fortified, I sat the chauffeurs down at our table and joined them for the first course (which was about £7 per head) and some nice wine (only marginally cheaper) ready for say an hour and a half of conviviality before having to look after the cutting of the cake and the speeches.

The oldest of the chauffeurs asked us a strange question … "d'you two expec ter git paid for this?"

Taken aback slightly, the Disc Jockey and I chorused "Well, of course we do!. This is a top class hotel".

"Well – do the 'otel expec ter git paid?"

"Strewth" I replied, "I should hope so! The food is about £40 per head, the drinks all night will be more and then there's the disco, the flowers, the cake … The bill will be in thousands. Why are you asking these questions?"

"Cos we ain't been paid" he retorted. "We've bin cartin this lot round London all day in my Rolls and these two fellas' cars, and none of us as bin paid. We've bin finished for two ours an we still ain't got our money".

"Oh, You'll get it chum", I said soothingly, "relax and enjoy your grub".

"Old on. Old on" he came back at me, "would you be surprised to 'ear that we picked up this lot from a two-pand-ten a night lodgins in Wandswerf?"

"What?" I gasped.

"Well … say seven pand-ten a night".

"Honestly?"

"I'm telling you" he insisted.

Folks from a Wandsworth lodging house booking a £9,000 wedding reception? I got worried and shot off for the Head Waiter.

He came reluctantly – he was busy after all looking after his valued customers, and I said to the chauffeurs, "Tell this chap what you've just told me, fellows".

They did, with a few more choice details, and I saw him go white. White as the chauffeur's collar. Whiter.

"Gaw'd elp us" he moaned, and staggered off in the direction of the Manager's office.

While the beautiful fish course (Another £7 per head) was being served, I asked the chauffeurs what they could do in such cases. I was thinking in terms of a Hire Cars Protection Association which could fight their legal claims for them. Their replies surprised and interested me.

"Well we frett'n ter call in the law an that often works. If it don't, we actually get the coppers, and that often works. An if that don't work ter-night we're gonna chuck the Bridegroom right froo that bleen't window".

I began to wonder whether this was a suitable environment for a six by-pass heart patient like myself but thoughts of leaving this sinking ship were banished by the appearance of the really gorgeous (£20 per head) main course.

While the Chauffeurs, Disc Jockey and I were tucking into this, our half empty table became the "office" for some high flowing financial discussions between the managers and some snappily dressed Nigerians brought over discreetly ("don't upset the Bride") from the top table.

We gleaned that the usual deposit cheque for £4,500 had not only been delivered very late on Friday evening but now on close examination had been found to be drawn on an obscure Nigerian bank. We also heard one of the snappy dressers offer his cheque guarantee card (£50 cover); and another offer to "take the Manager on a tour of the West End's Bureaux de Change, cashing £200 at each against his Barclaycard".

40

It nearly put us off our food.

At the appearance of the sumptuous dessert (at £6 per luscious plate) I came up with one of the sort of Ben Sullivan suggestions for which I was well known in the Bank. "Head Waiter" I said "they'll be expecting me to do the cutting of the cake and the speeches soon – and be asking for your £36 a bottle Champagne to be served". (He went that terrible white again). "Shall I vanish for a while until you sort something out? They won't start anything without me I should think".

He saw the logic of this and immediately agreed, so I slipped into the Kitchens. Time dragged in there, but sure enough after about ten minutes I heard a West African voice enquiring, "Where is that man in de red coat".

I hid in a cupboard!

A full thirty minutes later the cupboard door opened to reveal a determined looking Head Waiter.

"Do yer cutting the cake" he snapped, "an then open the bleedin Ball straightway".

"No speeches?" I queried, approvingly.

"No speeches, no drinks and don't let 'em actually cut inter the cake; they ain't 'aving that either!"

I paused as I went back in; the Banqueting Room looked different. No flowers, no wines – all gone.

"Urry up, mate" urged the Head Waiter.

"Ladies and Gentlemen" I called hurriedly, "the Bride assisted by her Bridegroom will now cut the cake".

This done, by a still radiant Bride and old Smiler, I moved them over to the dancing space and asked the guests to given them a welcome as they opened the Ball. Then invited everyone to join them.

Then I went home and was paid later by the hotel.

Note 1.

The Hotel had acted sensibly I think both in cutting their losses and in allowing the guests to stay for dancing. That was costing nothing extra whereas any attempt to evict the rather large guests might well have resulted in damage to the premises! It could also have ruined the greatest day of her life for the Bride, whom we all believed to be a completely innocent party. (As far as I know, she probably felt that the procedures – no speeches, no drinks after the meal, flowers taken off early – were routine at wedding receptions).

Note 2.

In a conversation with the General Manager of the hotel during a subsequent engagement, he told me gratefully that my weighing up of the situation and my actions on the eventful Saturday had saved the hotel a few thousand pounds. I had a momentary vision that an offer of a complimentary weekend at the hotel for my wife and myself was about to materialise … but he merely said, quietly and very sincerely, "Thank you".

30. Count your blessings

Every toastmastering job is different – because people are different. Some jobs are more different than others though; for instance a deaf and dumb wedding.

As usual, I had no idea that a wedding reception I'd accepted at the Naval and Military Club was any different from other weddings until I got there. "Deaf and Dumb!" I said to the organiser "How am I able to work if they can't hear me?"

"They'll watch your lips", she explained "and of course, lots of their relations and friends are "hearing" people. You'll manage Mr Sullivan, don't worry".

I <u>was</u> worried however as I tried to plan ahead. How would I attract attention if most of the guests couldn't hear my gavel? What would happen during the speeches? Would my "joke" telegrams be wasted?

Action is the best counter to worry however and action was near – the guests were arriving.

They'd arranged for a half-deaf Indian chap to stand alongside me during the Reception to act as an interpreter. After a very short time I began to wish to hell that they'd left me on my own!

Looking squarely at each couple as I'd been instructed, I'd say, with exaggerated lip movements "MAY – I – HAVE – YOUR – NAMES – PLEASE". Reading my lips they'd answer in high falsetto tones, something like "MIS-TEER AND MRS YAHOONG" (which I'd correctly assumed to be "Mr and Mrs Young") only to have to listen to the interpreter make it "Mr and Mrs Young". It could have been very embarrassing – but it wasn't, because the Indian, the Guests, the Hosts and myself all laughed at ourselves. Laughter was our common language.

Some of the biggest laughs came with the arrival of the "hearing" guests. To my slow moving lip question "MAY – I – HAVE – YOUR – NAME – SIR?" I'd get an amused smile and an answer in perfect English like, "Certainly old boy. We're Mr and Mrs Charles Brown and this is our daughter Fiona".

Somehow the Indian and myself got through the four hundred names without his knowing I wanted him to go away (how can you even hint to an afflicted chap who's doing his best for you) and I gave him a large glass of champagne.

Three quarters of an hour of cocktails and canapés followed in a hugely animated and happy manner. It was interesting to see how the faces of people who can't speak light up on occasions like this and how frequently they use their hands. It made the wedding seem even jollier than more normal weddings.

Different problems need different solutions. When the time came for the cutting of the cake I stood on a chair and waved to attract attention. Then the Bride and Bridegroom stood on chairs too and then cut into the top tier of their cake instead of, as usual, the bottom.

It went as well as at a normal wedding and I felt strangely affected as I looked down at the sea of slightly different faces. At least, I thought, they could <u>see</u> that part of the proceedings and enjoy it.

The next part, I felt was going to be more awkward. The Best Man was going to make a speech – the only speech of the day.

I asked him to stand on a chair to speak and he agreed willingly. He then produced a roll of paper, like the ones on the old adding machines, on which he'd written his speech in one long line. He read the speech from the roll, unwinding it as he did so and motioning to me to start passing the ribbon around among the deaf people assembled in front of us.

It was a delightful idea and within a few moments the ribbon snaked for yards with perhaps forty people reading different parts of the speech, laughing and gesticulating as deaf and dumb people do as they read the jokes the Best Man had cracked a few seconds before.

As I looked at these folk, deprived of the pleasure of hearing music, laughter, and the voices of loved ones, I wondered what life must be like for them. Even the thought of it must have affected me because suddenly I was aware that some of the guests had gone quiet and were nudging the others, pointing up to me with their eyes. Yes, the Toastmaster's eyes were filled with tears which threatened to jerk loose any second! Disgraceful really – but there you are; it <u>was</u> damned sad.

Count your blessings, folks. If you and your kids can see and hear and talk, you've a very lucky family.

31. Ask a busy man

I was once booked as Toastmaster at two evening Receptions for a hero of mine – Mr Lee Quan Yew, the Prime Minister of Singapore, who'd cleared his territory not only of communists but litter, graffiti and chewing gum too!

Round the small Reception room were beautiful flowers of a type I'd never seen and I mentioned to my hero that I loved them.

"They're Malaysian orchids" he told me. "They grow like weeds out there and last for six weeks as cut flowers". Then he added, "I'll have a couple of bunches wrapped for you to take home".

Overwhelmed at this kindness from a world leading figure, I thanked him profusely.

He then capped everything by promising to bring for me, at the second Reception, one month hence, some of Singapore's superior "Double" orchids which, he said, "would knock today's ordinary ones into a cocked hat".

My wife went crazy over the "ordinary" orchids when I presented them to her "with the compliments of a Prime Minister" but neither of us could really believe that the great man, with perhaps ten thousand problems to solve in the next four weeks, would then remember to bring some more, superior, orchids half way across the world for some little housewife in Kent!

However, as I entered the same room for the second Reception, the Great Man greeted me warmly and, pointing to two large bouquets of the most colourful flowers I've ever seen, said "I've brought the flowers for you".

If you want something done – ask a busy man.

32. Caruso in the red

One evening at the Strand Palace a quick glance at the Toast List revealed that the Loyal Toast was to be proposed by the Toastmaster. This was highly unusual; the Loyal Toast is normally given by the President, Chairman, Master or whoever is in the 'Chair'.

I pointed out this apparent clerical error to the organiser, expecting him to confirm that the Chairman would in fact propose "The Queen", but he replied that there was no mistake – the Chairman wanted the Toastmaster to do it.

I never argue with a direct order from those who are paying me, so I accepted the instruction. The thought also entered my rather big head that this time, the Loyal Toast would be submitted properly.

My readers will of course know when the Loyal Toast is to be proposed with musical honours, the proposer should stand to attention, <u>leaving his glass on the table</u>, pause for silence and then cry two words only. "The Queen". The drums of the orchestra should then roll for sufficient time for the guests to stand to attention, <u>glasses on the table</u> and then (ideally) as the orchestra starts the National Anthem the whole assembly should sing it. Only when the Anthem is concluded should the glasses be raised to the lips and the Toast drunk.

In practice, this rarely works. It takes a Chairman of very firm character to confine himself to two words and an audience of marked musical inclination to burst into song. He is more likely to say (holding his glass high in the air) "My Lord, Ladies and Gentlemen, I have the honour to propose the First Toast of the evening to that Gracious Lady Her Britannic Majesty the Queen (26 words) and <u>they</u> are almost certain to rise, glasses and all, shout "The Queen" and (horror of horrors) start drinking whilst the National Anthem is being played. They are unlikely to start to sing, except perhaps at the, "Send her victorious" stage, which, as becomes apparent to them all, is pretty pathetic. Their faces show clearly they wished they'd started earlier.

A lot depends on the Chairman and I find if I can persuade him (be he Duke or dustman) to do all the correct things and then with his wife sing right from the start of the National Anthem (letting the microphone pick up their voices) then things <u>can</u> go well; the assembly straightaway copy the actions and the singing.

Rarely, however, is it done perfectly – but by the blood of my Blarney ancestors it was going to be tonight. I'd do all the correct things and start the singing for everyone to follow. Then, because of my awful voice I'd fade, unnoticed by the assembly, and let them finish.

When the sweet course was cleared and the waitresses had been shepherded from the Hall, I gave three firm bangs on the table with the gavel. Then doing my best to look upright and imposing, I waited for complete silence.

When this was achieved, I proclaimed "The Queen".

Right on cue the drums rolled, the guests stood to attention and the orchestra commenced the National Anthem. I started to sing, in a very loud and clear but untrained and untuneful voice, "God Save our Gray-shush Queen, long live our no..." The guests weren't joining in! I flashed a panicky glance round the sea of faintly surprised faces "... ble Queen, God Save our Queen". Still only the one awful voice. A feeling of panic was welling in the singer but the band (the rotters) were starting to grin – especially the fat drummer. "Send her victor-ee-ous, happy and glor-ee-ous", I croaked on – (dare not stop. It would have been disloyal to the Queen) "Long to-oo ray-een over us, G-od (here I failed horribly to reach the high note) "Save the Queen".

At last it was over. Not one of the stinkers had joined in at any part of the Anthem. Many were still blanching a little, and the drummer was wiping his eyes.

"Thank you, Toastmaster" said the Chairman – with a nearly straight face.

"Wiv a voice like 'at you oughta be at Covent Garden" said the fat drummer, " – on a blee'nt fruit barrer!"

---

33. Unkind strangers

My front lawn is shielded from the street by a rhododendron hedge, thirty feet across, seven feet high and four feet wide. From it and obtruding well into the lawn used to be the stump of an old walnut tree with a circumference of some twelve feet.

It had to go if I was to have a really nice square and level lawn. I therefore devoted my spare time to chopping, digging and pulling to get it out, roots and all. Absolutely exhausting work it was too.

I was then left with a minor bomb crater some five feet deep which friends advised me to fill with earth and stones, topping up as necessary as everything settled. This, to my surprise took some months because every weekend I would find that the previous weekend's topping material had settled so far down that it had to be re-topped.

Ultimately, heaven be praised, the subsidence stopped and I had a nice bare plot of earth, some two yards square, ready to be added to my lawn.

With such a small area to cover, I decided to aim for perfection. This spot, so hardly won would be as smooth and level as a billiard table. It would be overlaid with the richest, composted soil, sieved through the finest gauge and spread with loving care. On this would be broadcast, at exactly one and a half ounces per square yard, the same grass seed as had been used on the rest of the lawn.

Then, to protect my masterpiece from greedy birds, I would insert very thin sticks, about five inches long at six inch intervals across the patch and join these, meticulously, with black thread. I would do my best, no matter how long it took – and even if I had to put the seeds in one at a time.

Imagine my satisfaction, therefore, when at the end of one long autumn day, I finally finished the task. I'd done my best – and it showed.

My proud wife rewarded me with a cup of tea and I sat in my favourite chair, looking through the window. Frankly, I was admiring my work ...

A noise and a quick movement in the street caught my attention. Some twenty yards down the hill a large black dog, which I'd never seen before, was chasing an equally unknown cat. Both were travelling very fast indeed!

Suddenly the cat veered to the right – into my garden. So did the dog. Then the cat shot across the lawn, smack into the middle of my freshly sown masterpiece, executed a skidding turn, and catapulted back into the street. AND SO DID THE DOG.

The last I saw of these two unkind strangers was a flurry of rear legs, tails, sticks and black cotton thread going back down the hill at fifty miles an hour!

Why did they pick on me? I've always been kind to cats and dogs.

34. The bastian's bofor

With the defeat of the Germans in Europe, there came the task of closing down the Allied Forces bases all over the Mediterranean. L.S.Ts. were particularly suitable for this job.

One base which needed clearing was at the port of Bastia in Corsica from whence the Americans wished to clear a mass of broken down jeeps, lorries, guns, aircraft tenders and other equipment.

My ship, H.M. L.S.T. 77 was sent to help and we found the loading was being directed by a great big, black and bullying American army sergeant who, while pushing his fifty strong gang of German and Czechoslovak prisoners of war to the limit, certainly got things done. We, in fact, stood somewhat in awe as, like a slave-master he made his men drive, push and manhandle the sometimes very heavy and awkward vehicles up our ramp, on to

the lift, out on to the upper deck and then as far aft and tight as he could cram them. The usual procedure was to drive or push them until they crashed in to the vehicles already parked, when he would yell, "Stop".

Things proceeded well and quickly and the upper deck was soon half filled with a motley collection of vehicles, tightly packed, all facing fore and aft.

Suddenly, there was a knee jerk reaction from my crew. A mobile Bofors Gun had, presumably to save space, been parked "sideways!"

We'd recently seen a Canadian soldier squashed to death by a tank which had broken loose in the Tank Space during heavy weather and we decidedly didn't want this Bofors Gun moving from side to side as our ship rolled – which the shallow-drafted L.S.T's were very prone to do!

I looked at the Navy boys and they looked at me. That gun would have to be manoeuvred to face fore and aft, now, before any more lorries were pushed up; otherwise we might have a very dangerous job later, at sea.

I therefore stepped forward and, in a very friendly manner, said to the Sergeant, "Excuse me, old boy, would you mind turning that gun fore and aft? You see, if we start rolling …"

"You mind your own business" he interrupted rudely, "I'm loading this ship!"

This, of course, was no way for a Sergeant to talk to an officer – especially in front of that officer's men, some of whom started to grin.

"Keep calm Ben" I said to myself "be British".

To the Sergeant, who was also smirking, I then said, "Excuse me, I think you misunderstand our way of doing things. I asked you to move the gun, but I was really telling you! Now, move it round – immediately!"

"And you keep your …ing mouth shut" was his reply as he turned to harangue his slaves again.

This time a couple of my matelots actually laughed. It was a bit embarrassing and I didn't really know what to do for a moment or two; but then walked forward, which both the sailors and the Sergeant took as a sign of defeat – the latter making some sneering remarks.

My loyal Leading Seaman, 'Chalky' White, followed me to see if he could help. "Just keep the lads here, Chalky" I murmured.

Moving to the f'castle, I called down to our armed guard, standing on the ramp, "Nothing more to come on board until you hear from me, <u>personally</u>" – and received his comforting "Aye, aye, Sir."

I then walked back to the Sergeant and the sailors, saying nothing and just watching as the "slave" prisoners of war pushed and shoved the stream of broken-down vehicles into the mass on the upper deck.

Suddenly, however, there were no more vehicles and the Sergeant rushed forward to the lift, screaming abuse at his terrified slaves there. Then down to the ramp where he carried on screaming at his other men.

I'd followed him down and felt that now was the time to calm him a little.

"Sergeant" I volunteered, "There's no more coming because I've stopped them. Now …" I added with appropriate hand signals "if you care to turn that gun fore and aft, I'll give the order to re-start loading."

Round two to the British Navy, I felt; but no, the so and so wouldn't admit defeat.

"I'm seeing my Colonel about you" he roared, and ran ashore.

"I'd like to see your Colonel too" I called and followed him along the quay past a long line of vehicles waiting to embark, until abruptly, he turned into a small hut. When I reached it I could hear him shouting most disrespectfully at his Colonel.

The Colonel, noticing me, came over and to my horror, whispered, "Please don't upset this man, he's my best loader."

Shaken, I whispered back, "And would you please tell your best loader not to upset me, Sir. On that ship, he does as <u>I</u> tell <u>him</u>."

"He'll never do that" he said dismally.

I think that remark turned something in my brain as I then heard myself, somewhat untypically, delivering an ultimatum.

"Then you can tell him Sir, that if the gun is not moved in three minutes – it's going over the side!"

The Sergeant laughed unbelievingly (he thought I was bluffing – and, in truth, I wasn't sure myself) and followed me back to the ship, over the ramp up the lift and amidships to the group of prisoners and sailors waiting there).

"Leading Seaman White," I barked, "get your team to take down four of the deck stanchions and guard rails, there."

This was done, quickly and with good humour; the lads were on my side after all!

My next order shook Chalky a little. "If the gun is not moved in one minute, push it over the side."

"Yes, <u>Sir</u>!" beamed Chalky.

There followed a very tense thirty seconds with the Sergeant (hesitant now, but still sneering) the prisoners and the sailors all staring at me with great intensity.

The civilian inside me probably wanted to give in at that moment, but the British Navy in there wouldn't stand for that. With twenty seconds to go, looking fiercely into the Sergeant's eye, I gave my best remembered command of the war. "Chuck the gun overboard!"

And, with a whoop of joy, Chalky and co. did just that!

Bully boy, horrified at last, ran to his Colonel. I, exhilarated but worried, reported to my Captain.

The Captain backed me fully.

"Quite right" he proclaimed. "Removal of hazardous cargo. We'll sail immediately."

And we did – leaving a great line of broken-down vehicles stretched out along the quay, and the Bofors Gun somewhere in the harbour.

I never heard another word.

35. Porridge

Whilst the guests at a Banquet are having their food, (one portion of everything served by a waiter to every ten coverts) I'm usually at my own little table in a corner (with as much as I want of everything, served by my own waiter).

Often my table forms a meeting place for a group of waiters "resting" between serving and clearing and we talk of this and that; last night's guests, the unions, religion and so on.

One evening the conversation centred on a supervisor well known on the banqueting circuit, who that day had been sentenced to eighteen months in prison for failing to pay Income Tax on "tronc" money (which some of the boys were saying he should have shared out among his waiters).

Some were of the opinion that he deserved all he got; others were more sympathetic. All agreed that this particular chap wouldn't enjoy prison life.

My bewilderment at hearing such unanimous and seemingly expert judgement must have shown on my face.

"I know wot I'm talkin abart" said a tall gaunt faced wine-waiter, reading my thoughts, "I've done free lots of porridge".

"So 'ave I" chorused others – all probably laughing inwardly at the instinctive very, very slight pressure I put on my wallet pocket.

It turned out that of the five of us, I was the only one who had not "done time".

I felt quite a cissy – but comforted myself with the thought that I had after all served eighteen months in the Bill Office of the Bank of England.

36. Some wedding!

Wedding receptions are some of the nicest things that happen to Toastmasters. I've officiated at hundreds of them; Christian, Jewish, Greek, Chinese, Arab, Italian and Indian and greatly enjoyed nearly all of them.

They've been at the great hotels, clubs and nicest of all, at private homes. The job has given me privileged entry into the homes of the famous (and sometimes the infamous) at a very special time in their lives – their daughter's wedding. In the main they treat me like a relative, and in fact I feel like one, zipping a bride's gown, washing a page boy's dirty knees and so on and, more often than not, calming either Mum or Dad down a bit. It's amazing, and comforting to find how families are nearly all the same and that many Dads have saucy daughters!

My first wedding was for a Deputy Chief Cashier's daughter (he didn't know it was my first but luckily it went off beautifully) and I have of course done scores of Bank weddings since – enabling me to meet and make friends with more Bank families at all levels than most Bank men. (Some of the nicest families I've met, incidentally).

Jewish weddings have provided some of the most spectacular (and exhausting) memories. One Host I remember paid the four lead singers from "Fiddler on the Roof" their full cabaret fee to sing "Sunrise, Sunset" just for the <u>entry</u> of the Bride and Bridegroom (as they did for the Bride and Bridegroom in the show). You know of course, as "with it" readers, that this song has lines like "Where is the little girl I carried?" "Where is the little boy at school?" "When did she grow to be a beauty?" "When did he grow to be so tall?" All good stuff – nearly everybody crying.

If asked at any wedding, which was my best wedding ever, I tactfully say, "this one" and in some ways it is true, but I suppose really my best wedding (next to my own) was that of Lieutenant Astor to a Miss Drummond.

George Cole, ex Buckingham Palace and Bank rang me at one day's notice to ask if I could do this one. I <u>was</u> free but I had arranged to take my wife out on one of our rare excursions together … "Bring her" said George, "be at Hever by 2.30 pm tomorrow".

The next day was a beautiful one for a wedding and after a nice drive to Hever where we saw crowds of people, we asked the local policeman (wearing medals and white gloves) where the Reception would be. He pointed to a big gate and we went through to find, glorious in the sunshine, the magnificent and romantic Hever Castle – once home of Anne Boleyn, now that of the Astor family. Yes! Lieutenant Astor was Lord Astor's grandson and he was marrying the daughter of Major Drummond, owner, I think of Harvey's Bristol Sherry.

The wedding was at the groom's house Hever instead of at Bristol, for understandable romantic reasons.

The butler gave my wife and me a most friendly and interesting tour of the Castle, so that I could answer the guest's questions where necessary, and then the Bridal party arrived back from the church. Gorgeous bride, handsome groom, each with really nice, kind relaxed parents.

The guests arriving largely by Rolls Royce and helicopter streamed colourfully over the castle drawbridge into a courtyard where each couple was given two glasses and a bottle of champagne with which to occupy themselves as they queued to be announced at the Reception.

The Reception, by the Bride and Bridegroom only, was in a large hallway absolutely full of beautiful flowers – a perfect backcloth for the handsome and happy pair. My recollection (probably influenced by my Irish steak of exaggeration) is that I announced no more than ten Misters and Missuses, all the rest being, "their Excellencies "Their Graces" "Lord and Lady" "Sir and Lady", all bubbling with good humour.

Having been received, the guests passed through a long picture gallery over the moat out on to the sun lit lawn, where the full orchestra of the Grenadier Guards was playing, into a great marquee, the decor of which rivalled the Mansion House, chandeliers included, where they found a bar about the size of the Bill Office at the Bank of England.

After a very convivial half hour or so at the bar they were invited to take their places at the tables for the Wedding Luncheon. Forty round tables, ten couverts each, between the flower bedecked, nylon covered, tent poles and on each table a vase containing a pyramid of tightly packed golden roses. I love colour and this was a feast of it. The hats, the dresses, the flowers, the golden chairs, the lawns, the Guardsmen's tunics and sunshine. I was really enjoying this wedding.

After a most sumptuous lunch, the cutting of the cake. The young couple climbed on to the rostrum and with his Army sword they cut into the bottom tier of the vast edifice. Three waiters then carried it away – it was about as big as a Concorde tyre and weighed 168 lbs – and then we were ready for the speeches.

I made the longest one – "Your Excellencies, Your Graces, Ministers, My Lords Ladies and Gentlemen, pray silence for the toast to the Bride and Bridegroom proposed by the right Honourable the Lord Cowdray of …" (28 words) and then his Lordship mounted the rostrum, raised his glass and cried, "The Bride and Bridegroom" (4 words). Slightly shaken, I then made the second longest speech, "Pray silence for the response by your Bridegroom, John" (9 words).

John left his lovely bride's side for a moment, and with a huge smile said, "I thank you" (3 words). Tumultuous acclamation for this fine example of brevity and then there was about an hour to spare before the departure of the happy couple.

I have three memories of that hour. Firstly my very literal acceptance of the hostess's instruction to help myself to the fabulous food; it was out of this world and I sampled everything! Secondly, my encounter with my friend the butler, in the picture gallery, when after looking at the signatures on some of the pictures I pointed to the word "REMBRANDT" and said to him "This <u>must</u> be a real one, being here?" "Of course", he said, his nostrils twitching ever so slightly.

"And that Picasso, that Monet and Constable?" said I, pointing to the various treasures. He nodded.

"Strewth" I said, thinking of the £3 – reproduction of "The Haywain" in my passageway, "how much is this lot worth?" About three and a half million" he said.

Three and a half million for pictures in a passageway! "Where do they get their money from now they've sold "The Times?" I enquired. "The Times" he said scornfully, "Was just a loss-maker, they kept it going for prestige purposes".

"How do they manage then?" I asked.

He explained "One of their ancestors Waldorf, was a fur trapper in Canada and the U.S.A. He used to sell his own and his trapper friends' furs. He started trading posts, distribution centres, hotels (you've heard of the Waldorf Astoria) and shipping companies. He spent some, saved some, and bought land with the remainder. Do you know the land he bought?" he asked with a twinkle in his eye.

"Tell me" I said.

"Well – it's now called New York. This family are the ground landlords for New York".

Fantastic. Just get yourself born an Astor and live on the ground rents for New York!.

My third memory is that of our Hostess thanking me for asking my wife to keep an eye on the deserted swimming pool during the cake cutting ceremony and speeches, in case one of the children fell in. "Thank God you did" she said, "She's almost certainly prevented a terrible accident".

It was all news to me of course. My wife (womanlike) had crept up to view the proceedings, just out of sight in the bushes round the pool exactly in time, as fate would have it, to grab a young four year old who was running full tilt into what he probably thought was a paddling pool.

Ah! Well! That's life.

Then it was time for the departure of the Bride and Bridegroom.

I usually ask the guests to "…assemble outside the house, around the car, ready to give your Bride and Bridegroom a really good send off". This time it was "Outside the Castle around the helicopter".

If you dear reader, intend to use a helicopter as your Wedding Coach, heed my advice and take off from a grassy or cemented pad. Avoid sandy gravel.

Mrs Astor couldn't heed my advice because her very full heart was set on taking off from the square (of sandy gravel) directly in front of the drawbridge.

"My" bride's wish is my command so that is precisely where she did take off.

Result, a fifty-foot cloud of dust with helicopter and castle disappearing from view.

Still, a great and lovely wedding – and good health to the Bride and Bridegroom.

═══════════

37. Robots cause unemployment

══════

Windows never fit sufficiently perfectly to stop the entry of some dust into buildings and they permit variations of light to enter according to changes in the time of day, season or weather.

Thus, when a factory was to be built in Felixstowe for the production of electrical meters (like the type found in most homes) and a dust free atmosphere and a constant, shadowless light was absolutely essential, some bright architect came up with the idea of a windowless factory with constant daylight lighting, the first such factory in Europe.

I was asked to officiate, as Toastmaster, for the official opening ceremony and journeyed from Liverpool Street Station with the Minister for Trade and a hundred or so slightly lesser mortals on a specially chartered train.

On arrival at the Company's private railway siding, we were greeted by the Company Chairman and the local Mayor and guided through a bright corridor, along an immaculate red carpet, into the dust free, shadowless factory.

The workers called from their labours and assembled in the sparkling new works canteen, gave us a cheer and listened attentively as the Minister made a nice speech and formally "opened" the factory (which had in fact been in operation for about three weeks). Most of the workers seemed quite thrilled to see a real Minister of the Crown, some Lords and so on and about ten of them even asked the 'umble Toastmaster for an autograph! (It's the red coat that does it!)

Then, the ceremony over, the workers went back to their benches whilst the visitors retired to cocktails and a splendid lunch.

I was given a small table alongside the great window of the upper floor canteen through which I could see almost the whole of the factory. As I sat there, enjoying the beautifully chilled gaspacho soup, followed by poached salmon and salad, and strawberries and cream, I remember thinking how nice it was, in exchange for making a few announcements, to be given a train trip in distinguished and fascinating company, an interesting visit to the sort of place I'd never normally see and now this really lovely lunch. Tomorrow too, would be just as nice in its own way; a Banquet for Her Majesty's Judges at Mansion House. Additionally my real job at the bank was an absorbing one (in Exchange Control) with different problems every day in very civilised company and conditions of service.

Then I suddenly thought of the poor devils at the benches below me. In their windowless, shadowless world one chap was taking a small metal fitting from a box on his right and another from a box on his left; placing them closely together in a heating machine, leaning backwards to allow a heat shield to come down between him and the machine, watching the two fittings fuse together, waiting for the shield to rise and then removing the fused fittings. Then taking another small metal fitting from the box on his right…

Near him was a girl, armed with a four pronged electrical screwdriver, who was tightening four screws into meters as they slowly passed by her on a production belt…

We Bank folk, perhaps advancing slowly in our index pensioned, civilised and mainly interesting jobs, able to look out of the Bank's windows and watch the sun, the clouds and the storms over our historic City, often have reason to worry and moan about our place of work … But let's not make too big a thing about it, eh?

---

38. Creating wealth

The ability to make something out of nothing is not given to us all. Those with it usually seem to accumulate a lot of money.

Take the time when the National Sporting Club gave a Celebrity Dinner for the British Lions Rugby Football team on their triumphant return from a wonderfully successful tour of Australia and New Zealand.

The bulk of the guests were directed to a pre-dinner reception on the sixth floor of the Café Royal and the V.I.P.'s (including the Lions, their manager and trainer) to the second floor.

The V.I.P's were to be received by the President, Sir Charles Forte and the Chairman, Sir Edwin (Ted) Leather. These two Knights, the General Manager and I met some fifteen minutes before the reception to run through the programme for the evening.

We were an experienced 'team', having stage-managed such functions before, and quickly covered the ground. One innovation for the evening was that the menus would take the form of plastic rugger balls which the guests could take home for their children and grandchildren.

For the top table, plastic was felt to be inadequate however and the General Manager told us that he had purchased four 'international match standard' leather balls for use there. He showed us one and we saw that it was a real craftsman's product, worth perhaps £15.00.

"May I have that ball?" asked Sir Charles and, on being given it, passed it to me with the request, "Please get the autograph of each member of the Lions as he arrives".

I did this with pleasure, proud to meet the hefty great heroes I'd read so much about, and was able to hand the ball back to Sir Charles with all the autographs listed neatly down one side; I even persuaded the captain, John Dawes, to sign at the head of the list.

I wondered briefly for which lucky Forte child this treasure was bound – a son, a nephew perhaps – but then my very full duties for the great banquet demanded all my attention and I forgot about it.

When dinner was over and we were at the coffee stage, Sir Edwin Leather called me over. "Before we start the speeches, I've got to auction that rugger ball" he murmured. "Can you get a bit of silence for me?"

A few bangs with the gavel and I got the by then rather boisterous, assembly quiet enough for Sir Edwin (an ace auctioneer) to make himself heard. "Mr President, My Lords and gentlemen" he said, with his very distinctive Canadian accent, "I've got an expensive rugger ball here, autographed by every single member of the British Lions Touring Team. I'm going to auction it and raise some funds for a sporting charity nominated by the team manager. Will someone open the bidding?"

"I'll give a hundred pounds" said Sir Charles.

"There's a start" smiled Sir Edwin. "Any advance on £100?"

In that sort of assembly there was, of course, and amid mounting tension (especially among the young Lions who weren't at all used to people bidding in £100 jumps for a rugger ball) we reached £900. It stuck there for a while.

"Going, going..." Sir Edwin was intoning when Sir Charles's quiet voice interrupted, "One thousand pounds". Great excitement, more tension at reaching this magic figure; and then suddenly, after a very discreet whisper from Sir Charles to Sir Edwin, the later announced, "John Dawes offers one thousand two hundred pounds". Cheers! Jeers! The poor Captain turned pale and started to whisper, "Steady, Sir Edwin..." Only to be restrained by a friendly hand on his shoulder. *Sir Charles's* hand.

Sir Charles then bid, "One thousand four hundred pounds!" More cheers and we wondered if anyone would top *that* bid.

Another whispered conversation between Sir Charles and Sir Edwin (which, remember, only a very few of us could hear) and Sir Edwin announced, "Barry Johns bids one thousand six hundred pounds!"

Excited applause and another "frightened" hero: Barry of course, had made no such bid.

The auctioneer let the victim stew for a minute, but before young Barry got too worried Sir Charles's quiet voice came in again. "One thousand, eight hundred pounds".

I think ultimately it was £2,000 that Sir Charles paid the Charity for the ball.

Two weeks later, in the same room, I was the M.C. at a Charity Dinner and Boxing Tournament arranged by the National Sporting Club for the King George V Fund for Sailors. Prince Philip was our guest of Honour and there were plenty of good-hearted business tycoons present to support him.

After the second bout, I had to invite Sir Edwin into the ring to auction – 'A rugger ball autographed by every member of the victorious British Lions team'.

Yes! It was the same ball and with some fine laughs, together with the normal tension and thrill of a good auction (all of which add to the enjoyment of an Evening Out) we raised another £800.

I must say I admire a man who, on the spur of the moment, can seize an opportunity to make a £15 rugger ball into a collector's item; raise its value further in an auction – which entertains some 700 guests; fight off fictitious bids (engineered by himself); and then pay £2,000 to a Charity in order to purchase his own brainchild (which he could have got for £15). And not content with that, to give the ball to another Charity who then raise a further £800 for themselves.

---

39. The whitebait festival

When the whitebait start arriving in the mouth of the Thames roughly at the beginning of September each year, the authorities at Southend-on-Sea hold a Whitebait Festival. I'm told that, to open the season, the local Mayor and a Bishop wade into the water and the Bishop gives a blessing on the fish.

On the same evening a fine banquet is held – probably the best in the Southend calendar. It ranks with the Colchester Oyster Banquet and the Sheffield Cutlers' Banquet. A London Toastmaster is engaged and the organisers usually manage to get a pair of really popular celebrities from the big City to be their speakers.

I did a couple of the Banquets, both of which stick in my memory. At the first one I called upon 'Miss Mary Spain' to respond for the Ladies, whereupon some five hundred people chorused, '*NANCY* Spain!' making me feel about one inch high. At the second, well … let me tell you of the "Whitebait procession".

The small group of V.I.P's who are to make up the 'Procession' are requested to remain in the cocktail bar after dinner is announced. When all the other guests have made their way to the table and are waiting behind their chairs, the Toastmaster forms the V.I.P's into a double file, according to rank, calls upon the Assembly to welcome them and then marches them into the Banquet to the sound, he hopes of enthusiastic applause. That sort of entry is always a thrill; the real start to the evening.

With the Whitebait Procession I had a problem. Because so many people wanted to attend the Banquet, the Hall was filled to capacity. The Top Table had therefore to be set very close to the wall (within, say, twenty-five inches), just leaving enough room for the guests to be seated and for a slim waitress to serve them.

Not enough room however for a Toastmaster to lead a double file procession along, especially with the guests *standing behind their chairs*, as they do when welcoming a Procession.

'There is only one way I can see to overcome this problem, Ladies and Gentlemen,' I explained to the V.I.P's when I'd formed them up outside the Banqueting Hall. 'After I've announced you, would you kindly march forward in pairs until we get to the top table and then, when turning left behind the other top-table guests, form a single file in the order in which you are seated. Thus Lady Bloggs will lead the file, followed by the Mayor, then the Mayoress, then myself (to be near the Chairman for Grace), then the Chairman, the Chairman's lady, the Guest of Honour and his lady, and finally Lord Bloggs".

They all agreed this was a good plan and the Chairman even congratulated the London Toastmaster for it. So we went to the entrance. Having signalled the orchestra leader to fade the music to a stop, I gave three bangs with my gavel. The Hall fell silent, the guests looked round expectantly and I called, loud and clear, "My Lords, Ladies and Gentlemen, be pleased to receive your Chairman and Mrs Smith, the Worshipful the Mayor and Mayoress of the County Borough of Southend-on-Sea, your Guests of Honour and your other Distinguished Guests".

The orchestra struck up with "See, the conquering hero comes" and we stepped forward to great applause, heading in pairs for the right hand end of the top table. Reaching it we paused and, like a well-drilled soldier, Lady Bloggs stepped forward, turned left and started to walk along behind the top table guests. The rest of us followed in absolutely correct order. My plan was going perfectly and for about two seconds I enjoyed a self-congratulatory glow.

One should never do that. It tempts fate! Suddenly there was a scream of panic from Lady Bloggs, three ahead of me, who seemed to have been spun towards the wall, followed by another from the Mayoress, whose pinky shoulders were suddenly bared to me! Then my red coat was jerked from my right shoulder and the Chairman's chain of office was hanging him instead of hanging *on* him!

All nine of us were caught up on a great fishing net, which, resplendent with sea-weed, glass ball floats and small lobster baskets, was decorating the whole of the wall behind the top table! As we, especially the blushing ladies, struggled to extricate buttons, clips, brooches, and chains from the net, the seaweed, the glass balls and baskets were tossed madly to and fro as though struck by a hurricane.

There was uproar in the hall, shouts, screams, laughter – and the good old band played on with the Conquering Hero (or did they change to the Fishermen of England?)

I was caught by one of my brass buttons but the moment I disentangled it, another one became caught as the elderly ladies thrashed about in blind panic, desperately trying to free their dresses from the monster net.

Eventually, by concentrating on the freeing of one person at a time, we got back to normal. By now, some of the guests were actually crying with laughter and it took quite a time to achieve a silence for Grace.

Altogether, a great start to the evening; I've rarely heard an assembly so cheerful and animated from the first course onwards.

It taught me a lesson too and these days, when ever I think everything is going perfectly, I listen carefully for that inner voice whispering 'Whitebait, Whitebait'.

---

40. It's not only terrorists you have to worry about!

Now I rate Mikhail Gorbachev as a truly great man, up with the Winston Churchills and Harry Trumans of the century. He, to me, is the man who freed my (and the world's) children and grandchildren from the threat of nuclear holocaust.

I was immensely proud, therefore, to be chosen for the task of introducing him on the occasion of his famous speech at Guildhall. So great was the pride, in fact, that when I'd finished, and realised that my announcement, televised to millions in Europe, particularly Russia, and the United States, had gone over very well, I hallucinated slightly for the only time in forty-five years of Toastmastering. Sheer relief, I suppose…

My most vivid memory of that outstanding day, however is of an incident a little later, when the time came for our distinguished visitor to process from the stage with the Lord Mayor and Prime Minister Thatcher.

They were preceded by the City Sword bearer, carrying the Sword of State and the Common Cryer, carrying the City Mace, this latter official being on the left, immediately in front of Mr Gorbachev.

As usual, the Common Cryer took the first few paces with the five-foot long, heavy Mace held high in front of him i.e., at the position of 'present'. Then as he descended the first step, followed perhaps too closely by the Russian Leader, he heaved it to the 'Slope' position on his left shoulder. Horrifically, as the shaft of the Mace was landing on the Common Cryer's shoulder, the crown on the top of it was coming down very fast towards Mr Gorbachev's shining, unprotected head – stopping perhaps an inch from it!

If that first step down from the stage had been an inch deeper there really would have been a very nasty accident.

We on his left must all have gasped and I'll never forget the Great Man's reaction. He turned to us very calmly, palms up, Jewish style, shrugged his shoulders and then gave us a beautifully mischievous smile.

It was marvellous; but my goodness only we few who saw it all happen knew how nearly History was changed that day.

41. Silly Billies

On March the 18th in the year AD 978, King Edward the Martyr, aged fifteen, was stabbed to death by Queen Elfrida's (his stepmother's) henchmen so that his stepbrother, Ethelbert the Unready, aged six, could accede to the throne of England.

The dastardly deed was executed treacherously while Edward was drinking to the health of his stepmother using the double handled Loving Cup which ensured that both his hands were innocently employed and he not in a position to defend himself.

Since then, in a ceremony thought to have been introduced by Queen Elfrida herself, to protect Ethelbert, guests at the great banquets in the City of London have "protected" each other whilst using the Loving Cup.

The Ceremony of the Loving Cup takes place after the Sung Grace which follows the meal, but prior to the proposal of the Loyal Toast.

The Master of the City Company, on introduction by the Toastmaster, then rises, holding a Loving Cup with both hands and turns to the guest on his right, who rises to face him. At the same time, the guest on his left stands back-to-back with the Master.

Thus we have three persons standing the 'Drinker', the 'Guest' who is to be toasted and the 'Guard' who is to protect the 'Drinker's' exposed back.

As the orchestra starts to play the much loved old drinking songs like 'Drink to me only with thine eyes' and 'Little brown jug how I love thee', the Drinker and the Guest bow to each other. Then with his right (or sword) hand, the Guest raises the cover (or lid) of the Loving Cup high into the air to prove he is not carrying a sword.

The Drinker then drinks a toast to the Guest and, having done so, wipes the lip of the Loving Cup with the napkin tied to one of its handles before the Guest replaces the cover.

Drinker and Guest then bow to each other and the Guest, taking the Loving Cup from the Drinker's hands turns right about to face the person on his right – who now becomes the Guest.

The former Guest, now holding the Loving Cup, becomes the Drinker, the former Drinker becomes the Guard and the former Guard, duty done, sits down.

This first Loving Cup is passed along to each guest on the right of the Master, who was the first Drinker. Immediately he has drunk to the Guest on his right and handed the Cup to him, he turns left and whilst acting as Guard, raises a second Cup and repeats the Ceremony with the person on his left (i.e. His former Guard).

As the Master, in conclusion hands the second Cup over to this Guest to start it off on its journey along the left of the top table, the 'Gunners' seated at the end of each sprig table start the Ceremony on their tables – where it passes to their left, up and round the sprig and back to the Gunner.

It takes about twelve minutes for the Cups to circulate to every person in the Hall and one can imagine, especially with guests who have already consumed a few other drinks, that some hilarious confusions can arise.

As Toastmaster, I do my best to avoid delays etc., by very quietly, before and during the Ceremony, instructing the first few people involved, knowing from experience that guests on the sprigs will watch and copy them.

At one important banquet, some years back, the first Guest was the wife of a Secretary of State, who after turning right and drinking to her husband, forgot to wipe the lip of the Cup before passing it to him. I was too late to prevent this but a moment later when it was <u>his</u> turn to make the traditional hygienic wipe and he also failed to do so, I was ready.

"Wipe the lip, Sir," I hissed, as he started to hand the Cup over.

He stopped, gave me a look, and then grabbing the napkin tied to one of the handles of the Cup, gave his <u>own</u> lips a thorough wiping!

Strangely enough, at the same Banquet the following year, another Secretary of State from the same Cabinet committed exactly the same gaffe!

Two silly B's from the same political party!

(In case you're thinking of asking Ben which one it was, be warned that he vows that his lips are sealed so tightly that wild horses would have to labour mightily to drag the truth from him. Ed).

---

42. Hopping mad

At the end of a great banquet it is sensible, for reasons of protocol, security and plain convenience to arrange that the Chairman and Principal Guests retire from the Banqueting Hall before the other guests leave their seats.

At the Lord Mayor's 'Semi-State' banquets (those to the Ambassadors, Bishops, Judges, Bankers, etc) at Mansion House, this is achieved by the Toastmaster's traditional announcement. 'Please to make way for The Right Honourable the Lord Mayor and the Lady Mayoress, the Sheriffs and their Ladies and the Principal Guests'.

The Toastmaster then draws the Lord Mayor's chair to the rear, and the City Marshall, having taken care of the Lady Mayoress' chair, leads them and their Principal Guests off, to the applause of the assembled company.

One night, at the conclusion of the Banquet to the Bishops, I experienced difficulty in pulling back the Lord Mayor's chair (or 'Throne'). It's a heavy great thing (weighing about two hundred-weight, I guess, some five foot high and two foot six inches wide, with carved, gilded wooden arms, plush velvet upholstery and mounted on four castors) so I pulled it hard – only to hear a shout of agony from the Lord Mayor!

Peering round the great edifice I glimpsed his pain-racked angry face.

'Are you all right, my Lord Mayor?' I queried.

'No, I'm not!' he snorted. 'You've pulled that, that chair right over my … foot'.

(I'm sure from his lip movements that he wanted to use a colourful adjective there, but remembered in time that the Most Reverend the Lord Archbishop of Canterbury was seated next to him.)

He must have had his right foot tucked behind the right front leg of the Throne and, when I pulled, it had gone right over his thin, buckled court shoe. It must have been agony for him.

'I'm very sorry, my Lord Mayor' I stammered, and again saw his lips forming a silent opinion about my parentage, 'I …'.

"This way, my Lord Mayor' boomed the City Marshall, saving any further embarrassment, 'Please follow on, your Graces, my Lords…'

So off went the Lord Mayor and his Principal Guests. The Guests walking, the Lord Mayor hopping, with the occasional stop to massage his foot.

The Toastmaster slunk off, the back way!

43. While London slept

After a Comedie Francaise Supper at the French Ambassador's Residence a very sweet elderly lady asked me if we could telephone for a taxi to take her home.

I knew from previous such requests that this <u>was</u> possible, but only if the customer was prepared to wait for at least half-an-hour. I therefore suggested that she sat on one of the great upright chairs in the entrance to the Residency, with a glass of champagne for company, while I asked the Residency staff to 'phone for a taxi.

Madame Marie Rambert (yes it was the founder of the Ballet Rambert) thanked me warmly and waited patiently in the big chair legs dangling, looking just like a little girl.

Each time I passed her in the next twenty minutes she gave me a lovely smile and I always said something like, "Won't be long now, Madame." I began to get a little worried about her, however, as she looked so small and frail in that great big chair – and the damned taxi was so long in coming.

When my wife arrived to collect me, I changed out of my red-coat and prepared to go; and the lonely little figure was still waiting in the hall.

"Madame" I said, bowing like a French diplomat, "It's some time since I've had the pleasure of taking a new girl friend home. May I give you a lift? My wife has brought the car up and she's not at all jealous."

My wife was of course thrilled to meet the famous lady. She had recently watched a T.V. programme about Madame Rambert and here was the star, in the back of our old Ford.

During the short journey to her home we naturally spoke to Madame about the ballet. She was so interesting to listen to that we continued talking on the pavement outside her house and while there I said I wondered if, like some athletes, ballet dancers stiffened up a lot once they stopped exercising regularly.

"I think they would" she said. "That's why I do my exercises every day". With this she performed an exquisite movement of her right hand to which we responded with a round of applause. Thus encouraged, she gripped the area railings, rose on her tip toes and did a couple of very high kicks and bends. More applause and we were rewarded by a few spins, a high leap and a perfect bow to finish; all with wonderful grace and style.

We treasure that moment – our own top-class little ballet show, on the pavement in Notting Hill just after midnight; and our ballerina was eighty four years old.

---

44. The other navy

Early in my naval career I served as the gunner on H.M. trawler "Ocean Brine" which used to patrol a sixty mile stretch of the North Sea escorting coastal convoys and keeping a look out for German planes and E Boats.

Our crew of twenty three was commanded by an Aberdonian skipper R.N.R. who was not a nice man at all. A pre-war trawler skipper he had during the thirties slump been unable

H.M.S. "Ocean Brine"

to get a job at sea and by the outbreak of hostilities had been reduced to serving as a labourer at Rank's Flour Mills in Hull. He was a very heavy drinker and, as it transpired, a crook.

Morale on board wasn't too high, principally because even two months after our commissioning, we still hadn't received permission to hold "Bond" on board. This meant that our crew, unlike those of the ships we worked with, were unable to obtain duty-free cigarettes.

Complaints to the Skipper produced promises to chase up the appropriate authorities – but as far as we were concerned he did nothing.

Our food wasn't all that marvellous either and what little we had was ruined by our cook, Jock Palmer, who was we felt sure a relation of the famous murderer, Palmer the Poisoner.

I was one of the chief moaners – especially about the food. So vocal was I on one occasion that the Leading Seaman responsible for ordering it suddenly threw two books at me, with the exhortation, "There's the Purser's Book, there's the Naffi Book, you do the bleed'nt ordering from nah on!"

"If I can't do it better than you" I vowed, "I'll eat both books."

I did my very best too, for the next two weeks, even making the supreme sacrifice for my shipmates by taking out a horse-faced girl from the Naffi so that we could get some luxury foods cheap.

But then we were dealt a terrible blow; a party of Supply Assistants from the Purser's Office ashore came on board with authorisation to check the ship's emergency stores. They were referred to me as I (a very simple A/B) was now apparently in charge of the ship's catering, and demanded to see the 56 pounds of butter, 48 cans of corned beef, 48 tins of condensed milk etc., that we were supposed to have in store.

We all denied ever having seen these (and we'd all been on the ship since its commissioning) but they produced receipts, signed by our drunken skipper which "proved" that the stores had been delivered to the ship.

No emergency stores could be traced, however, so I as "Catering Manager" was given an official reprimand and told that further stores would be delivered which should be locked away securely, with perishables being replaced regularly. The full cost of the new emergency stores would be charged to the crew by deductions from our food allowances over the next three months.

The crew went mad! Badly fed for months, they were now to suffer reduced rations for another three months! And all were convinced it was due to fiddling, either by the shore staff (who could easily sell canned food on the black market) or by the skipper.

A deputation was therefore sent to the skipper's cabin. Me!

Waiting until he'd bidden farewell to his lady-love, "Funfair Kate", the local tart, I entered the love-nest and went straight into my much rehearsed attack.

"Sir", I said, "we seamen and stokers have got to pay for the missing emergency stores, which you signed for but we've never seen."

"If I signed for them they came aboard" he growled.

"Well, Sir, you were blind drunk during those first few days and probably signed anything that was put in front of you. It's not fair that we should pay! We only get two shillings (10p) a day and you get twenty-seven (£1.35) and it's your fault. Don't you think you ought to pay, Sir?"

"Get out! Get out!" he roared.

I went out defeated, back to the boys, who'd heard the verbal exchanges between the skipper and myself (and probably many of Funfair Kate's low moans before that!) through the thin bulkhead which separated the skipper's cabin from our Mess Deck (both of which had previously formed the fish-hold). The boys were very unhappy and said so in a few words – which they repeated over and over again.

There was no alternative, however. We had to cut down severely in the next three months or we'd be in serious trouble. The Purser's Office said they'd delivered the goods and they had our skipper's signature for receiving them. No one would take our word against theirs.

Food was important to us in the freezing North Sea but I got the lads to cut down on Naffi luxuries like eggs, bacon and sausages and buy more staples like bread and potatoes from the cheaper Purser's stores. My romantic advances to the Naffi girl yielded dividends too in the form of the odd pound or two of cheese which she used to pinch from the store. I was also able to persuade all the crew except one to accept margarine rather than the more expensive butter for three months. I still remember being surprised that the lads should agree that one chap should keep on with butter; apparently he just couldn't face marge.

We also saved some expense by fishing ourselves, or cadging from local trawlers for whom I, supposedly, provided anti-aircraft cover. (In those days, 1940, we had one Twin-Lewis machine gun!) Additionally we sold some of the ship's ropes to a local fisherman, (reasoning that the Navy had swindled us so we'd swindle them) and the teetotallers amongst us started drawing the rum allowance (issued neat on the trawlers) and bottling it for a baker ashore who then gave us bags of his unsold rolls, old meat pies, etc.

We also saved some expense by fishing ourselves or cadging from local trawlers.

We therefore were managing somehow but one and all were waiting for release from our unfair burden – no one more so than the Catering Manager and Crook-in-Chief.

Then, with just a couple of weeks to go, some idiot threw every knife and fork overboard with the washing-up water. I went bananas at the prospect of having to pay to replace them from my hard earned savings and the miscreant immediately promised that next time he and his Watch went ashore, they'd all have fish-and-chip suppers in an Edinburgh fish café and pinch the knives and forks. The fact that the Catering Manager, later to be an honest Bank of England man, so readily agreed to this plan shows to what levels of desperation he'd been reduced. (And later probably made him a more understanding Exchange Controller!)

While we were in harbour during the final week of our sentence (we used to do six days at sea, two in harbour) the cook one day produced some boiled-white lumps of beef, wet mashed potatoes and "varnish" gravy as lunch for the watch-on-board. This included the skipper but, as he was away drinking with his equally obnoxious and drunken friend, the skipper of another minesweeping trawler, which was tied up two outside us, his portion of the gastronomic feast was shoved into the oven.

Some three hours later while I was in the galley with the cook, cutting green mould off some of the baker's old rolls, a young seaman from the other trawler climbed over to us with a message to the cook … .

"Your skipper seys 'ees missed 'is dinner so he wants a cornbeef sanwitch – quick" he said. This demand for a corned beef sandwich really got up my nose. We'd all forgone such luxuries for three months because of the skipper's drunkenness and here he was, demanding one! Didn't he realise we'd have to open a tin weighing ten pounds just to get his slice and then possibly have to sacrifice the rest. Why should we lose another £2 – ?

"No corned beef Jock" I ruled; "let him have the same as us."

Jock, a Glaswegian who'd suffered more than most of us at the hands of our monster, fully agreed.

"Tell him his dinner's in the oven and if he doesn't want that he can go and …" (here he referred to an hermaphroditic contortion)

I suspect that the puzzled messenger must have delivered the reply word for word for suddenly, we saw the skipper lurching over two trawlers towards us, in a mad temper.

"Where's my food?" he roared.

"Yer dinner's in the oven" snarled Jock, and gave the oven door a well practised kick which caused it to fall open.

"In the oven. In the oven," chanted the skipper, mimicking Jock's Glaswegian accent and grabbing the plate of congealed black from the oven, threw it, plate and all, over the side.

"That plate'll cost us one and six (7½p)" I wailed.

"One and six, one and six," he hissed, this time adopting my cockney tongue, "here goes another couple of one and sixes." (This time they were clean plates from the rack. Well fairly …clean …).

"You'll have to pay for those, Sir" I spluttered.

"Oh! You'll have to pay for those Sir" he repeated, throwing a frying pan (thirty bob or £1.50) a saucepan (ten bob or 50p) and a block of cheese into the harbour.

I was aghast, That cheese, especially, had cost me dear! Before I could say anything, however, he spun on Jock, who'd been watching with a contemptuous sneer. "Call yourself a cook?" he yelled "My daughter of eight could cook a better meal than you, you Glaswegian bastard."

Jock, who was tough, wore a razor blade in his cap and had an aversion to being called a bastard, sprang ferociously at the skipper, grabbing him by the neck.

I was horrified! Jock was attacking AN OFFICER! I grabbed at his arms and pulled him off. "Jock! Jock! Don't hit AN OFFICER" I bawled, "Report him, <u>report</u> him. I'll be your witness."

"You stay out of this" said the skipper, surprisingly "I like you. But as for this Glaswegian bastard … "

Jock went to spring again but this time I was between these two mad Scots.

"You can't keep calling people bastards Sir, especially your crew" I panted desperately "and if he reports you, I <u>will</u> be his witness."

"So you'll be his witness, eh?" he retorted. "Well, you're a cockney bastard!"

That did it. I dragged the unwilling Jock ashore to the Base Office where we reported all to a Commander Sinclair(who turned out to be the brother of Archibald Sinclair, the Air Minister).

Our statements, roughly the story you've just read, were typed by a demure little Wren, before whom I (a good swearer in front of the boys) found I just could not utter the word "bastard." Eventually the exasperated Commander had to snap (and it's one of those little moments one remembers throughout life) "O.K. Miss Green, so the skipper said to Sullivan 'Well you're a <u>cockney</u> bastard.'"

There then followed a very awkward month with the same skipper, before we were given a new very harsh one who told us he'd been instructed not to give us an inch – and then stopped our shore leave for two weeks just to show us who was boss. Jock and I then had to take a lot of stick from the rest of the crew who (as is the way of this old world), had quite forgotten that they'd put the bullets in for us to fire.

The old skipper was Court Martialled and dismissed the Service. (I think the authorities had been trying to "get" him for some time and we merely gave them their chance). He went back to fishing and, soon after, we read in the "Stornaway Times" that he was making £300 per week. (Worth £3,000 now?).

Jock and I immediately and rather cheekily wrote to him asking for some reward for helping him to get out and make money, but received no reply.

If he'd had any sense of fair play he would have rewarded the crew for he did indeed owe us something. We found that the tyke <u>had</u> received the Bond right from the start of the commission and had kept it all for himself – while his crew paid full price for their cigarettes ashore.

Now that, as Jock said (and forgive me ladies) was the action of a <u>real</u> bastard !

---

45. Learn to listen

Having "Prayed silence for Grace by the Reverend Chad Varah" on many occasions I read his life story in the Reader's Digest with great interest.

When next I met him, at a Banquet for the International Congress for the Prevention of Suicide, I asked him for his autograph. "My autograph?" he said, "Why should you want my autograph?"

I knew exactly why. I took a deep breath and said, "I've just read your story Sir. A good pal of yours committed suicide and you made a vow to try to help all would-be suicides. You then asked to be given a bombed-out church in the City with no parishioners so that you could concentrate on this work. You got it and on your first visit there you picked up a dirty old pre-war telephone lying in the bomb-rubble and asked the operator whether you could be given an easily remembered telephone number like the Police '999'. The church was in the Monarch Exchange area so you thought something like Monarch 9000 would be a good number. Then she asked if you were kidding and you rubbed away the grimy bomb-dust from the front of the 'phone and found that <u>was</u> the number you were using.

You thought it was a miracle – and so do I, Sir. Then you founded the Samaritans who have saved thousands of lives in the U.K. and whose work has been copied in most countries of the world".

"You can have your autograph" he said.

Remembering how I've sometimes been able to cheer people up or help them through a difficult patch, I then said, with my natural immodesty, "Can I become a Samaritan, Sir?" I think I'd be good at it".

"No thank you" he replied, "we wouldn't want you …"

This blunt reply from such a kind and holy man really startled me and although I tried not to look hurt, something must have shown on my face.

"Mr Sullivan" he added more kindly, when people are in a suicidal mood they need someone to listen whilst they pour it all out. They don't want to be cheered up or be given good advice; they just want someone to listen. You wouldn't be any good, you're a talker!

"Now if your wife would volunteer, we'd take her – she must be a good listener".

Some years later when talking to a friend who is a hypnotist it emerged that he was a member of the Bromley Samaritan team.

"Your boss shook me one night" I complained.

"You've actually met Chad Varah?" he gasped, as though I'd said I'd met the Pope.

"I certainly have" I said and with tongue in cheek, told him how my kind offer had been rejected.

"He was absolutely right, you know, Ben" he said, "you are definitely not the type."

"I know he was right" I admitted, "but surely if you've got someone who is willing to help, you should allow him to do so in some way".

"Well" he mused, "when we get emergency calls, we keep the patients talking until we can get a car to them which will bring them to our local Samaritan centre. Would you be willing to be a driver? We might call on you soon or never, dependent on the number of cases in your immediate neighbourhood. It could be at 3.00 am one day and we'd ask you to pick a patient up, keep him warm, listen to him and bring him to us quickly".

"I'd be glad to help", I said.

"O.K. Ben, I'll put your name on our list of drivers; and thank you for the offer – and Ben" he added, "Just keep your mouth shut …"

---

46. "I've got a King here, you know"…

Of the two hundred odd State Banquets and eighteen world Boxing Championships I've looked after, the greatest occasion must have been the Banquet on 6th May 1995 to celebrate "Victory in Europe + 50". Great in that it was not only attended by the Queen and nineteen members of the Royal Family but the Sovereigns and Heads of State of 60 other nations.

Each Sovereign or Head of State was, on arrival, placed in the care of a Corporation Escort (or Minder) whose duty it was to introduce him and his consort to the Lord Mayor and Lady Mayoress, Prime Minister and Mrs. Major; to see that they got a pre-dinner drink or two; to hold them back when "Dinner" was announced until all other guests were at their tables; to bring them in loose procession to my assistant and myself so that we could proclaim their names to the assembly; and then to conduct them to their seats and sit with them throughout the Banquet, attending their every whim.

For we two Toastmasters there was a slight edge to TIMING. We wanted no delay in getting the main body into Great Hall, followed by the members of the Royal Family

followed by the Sovereigns and Heads of State, followed, after a triumphal fanfare by Her Majesty the Queen.

Then, very unusually <u>before</u> Dinner, an extended Toast to "The Queen" by the Lord Mayor, the playing of the National Anthem and the Queen's gracious response. And finally, Grace by the Lord Mayor's Chaplain. Then Dinner.

To my great personal relief we achieved all these targets in good time. Our real worry had been that, had we been late, the millions of television viewers watching us would have switched over to that other new but vital Saturday event – the National Lottery!

There was just one last duty. As soon as Dinner was finished, and coffee and liqueurs served, we Toastmasters were to ensure that the Hall was cleared of waiters and silence achieved for the Sergeant at Arms and Common Cryer to announce, "You now have Her Majesty's permission to smoke".

We were ready with 3 minutes to go, when I saw a very strange and frightening thing. From the guest seated immediately on the Queen's left hand was rising a thick column of cigar smoke! Before our horrified eyes it slowly drifted up to the right and towards the Queen. Luckily however, assisted by a little fanning from us, it moved back to the left.

The culprit was King Hussain of Jordan – the most senior of the visiting Heads of State. How does one tell a King to "put his fag out"?

People nearby told me later that at that stage I looked just like the Horrified Butler in a Bateman cartoon; but something had to be done.

I therefore approached the King's minder, a General and former Governor of the Tower of London, who was seated between the King and Queen Noor.

"Excuse me, General" I said quietly.

"Why, hello Mr. Sullivan" he replied with a friendly smile, "hasn't it all been a lovely …"

"Sir", I whispered, "I wonder if you could tactfully request your charge to refrain from smoking for a few minutes until the Common Cryer gives Her Majesty's permission to smoke?"

The smile was instantly replaced by an expression of intense worry.

"I've got a King here, you know …", he stammered.

"Yes, I know Sir", but I think you ought to try …"

He then very slowly turned toward the King but, surprisingly, it was the King who spoke first and whatever he said immediately caused the muscles in the General's neck to relax. Obviously relieved at what he'd heard from the King he turned back to me and smiled.

"It's O.K. Mr. Sullivan, His Majesty heard you and has just reminded me that we had the Loyal Toast before the meal and it has been in order to smoke since then".

This was technically correct, of course, and I nearly retired from the fray but then decided to persist.

"I agree Sir, but come what may, the announcement will be made in about one minute from now and I just felt His Majesty might be very embarrassed if, as the Common Cryer is proclaiming, 'You now have Her Majesty's permission to smoke' he, seated next to HER, is observed to be puffing at a big cigar".

The King heard this too, luckily, and with a slight, friendly wave, very deliberately stubbed out the expensive cigar. Mission accomplished.

Nevertheless if I ever visit Jordan I think I'll go under an assumed name. The Tower is probably out of bounds, too.

---

47. Rosing to the occasion

During the Variety Club of Great Britain's tribute to the Queen Mother at Grosvenor House in her 90th Anniversary year, one of my duties was to call upon representatives of the companies/associations which were sponsoring the evening to come to the dais, where Her Majesty was standing in front of throne-like chair, so that each could present to her a single long-stemmed rose. Each rose was of a different variety and each stem had been carefully divested of every one of its thorns, so that no injury was done to the gentle, ninety year old hands.

As each rose was presented and accepted, the Queen Mother passed it from her right hand to her left. I then had to read the name of the next presenter, his Company and the variety of rose he was presenting, take the preceding rose from the royal left hand and place it delicately in an urn mounted on a pedestal behind us.

Speeches by Sir John Mills and Mr Eric (Miss World) Morley followed, leading up to an hour long, wonderfully staged, musical fashion show, depicting how a young couple met by the pool, courted at various venues, married and went on honeymoon – always accompanied by about a hundred bright young things, all dressed in the latest swim – dance – wedding – and honeymoon – wear, and all dancing and miming beautifully to the most popular and appropriate of the Bing Crosby, Frank Sinatra and Shirley Bassey recordings.

When the Fashion Show closed, my young Assistant and I had to lead the Royal Party out. They were to be escorted by Sir John and Lady Mills and Eric and Julia Morley.

I asked my Assistant to gather the nineteen roses (now sadly looking a tiny bit droopy) from the urn so that the Guest of Honour could take them back to Clarence House. He did this and then joined me to lead the Procession towards the exit.

As we approached the ceremonial staircase leading from the Great Room we were stopped by a small party of officials, who presented to the Queen Mother a most gorgeous

and large bouquet of colourful and long-stemmed roses, each of which rested separately upon a bed of soft white paper. It was about three feet long and two feet wide, too bulky for Her Majesty to carry up the stairway, so she handed it to me, so that as we all proceeded up the steps (to thunderous cheers from the thousand guests) and along the corridor, my Assistant and I were both carrying roses, out front.

Walking there, almost in a dream (what's Ben Sullivan, out of Hoxton doing here with the Queen Mum?) I heard our gracious guest discussing the colours of the roses, so I politely held the great bouquet well to my right so that she might more easily see them as she talked about them.

"Do you love roses too?" she called. I stole a glance over my shoulder, nearly tripping; was she asking me? She was…

I stopped and turned "Er – yes your Majesty, I do".

"But do you <u>really</u> love them, as I do?" she persisted.

"Oh yes, Mam, I <u>really</u> love them" I murmured, and then added (why I don't know but probably because my heart was telling me to) "In fact, I've got a most wonderful rose at home".

"You have?" she said, and perhaps thinking I patriotically meant the "Elizabeth of Glamis" rose, named after her, continued, "Which one is that?"

"My wife, Rosie, Mam" I said.

There was a silence during which it flashed in on me that I'd wrecked a career which had taken thirty-odd years to build, and then, with a lovely tinkling sound, she giggled. Like a school girl.

"Oh! How lovely" she choked, "how lovely".

Eric Morley gave me an almost imperceptible warning glance, as if to say "Don't push it" so we hastily moved out into Park Lane, where crowds had assembled to watch the departure. Quite a sight! The Royal limousine, the police escorts with blue lights flashing and the whole of the south bound carriageway jammed behind them.

We handed the flowers to the chauffeur and stood there bowing as the country's favourite grandmother glided by. She stopped, shook my hand (I've never washed it since!) and said, "Thank you, lovely, quite lovely!"

So I got away with my impulsive little indiscretion that time – and have been a good boy since.

48. A happy incident

After printing expensive invitation cards for a dinner in honour of a visiting Russian shipping delegation, a great ship-owners' association found that the Russians had come to the U.K. without dinner-jackets.

The invitation cards stipulated "Dinner-jackets" and, as there was no time to reprint them, they were altered in ink before despatch. This, though most regrettable, worked well in every case but one ...

The first I knew of the alteration was when, having announced some fifty lounge-suited guests, I turned to see a chap in a dinner-jacket. "Good evening, Sir," said I, innocently, "May I have your name?" "No you damn well can't" he snapped. "Why are all those men in front wearing lounge suits? I'll bet I'm the only one in a dinner-jacket. Where's that stupid Secretary?"

(The Secretary, who'd been standing close the President slid into a side room).

The peppery person pushed past me and protested to the President. "I'm not standing for this" he snorted. "Why wasn't I told of the change?"

"We altered all the Invitation Cards", stammered the President, clearly upset. All the previous guests had shaken his hand warmly and wished him a happy evening. Why should this one be so nasty – and where was that flaming Secretary?

"Show me where that card's been altered" retorted the disgruntled guest, waving a card as clean and free of alterations as a letter from a Court of Law, "I'm going home!"

Something in the poor President's face and in the sad eyes of the Secretary now peeping through the door, goaded me into action. I stopped the nasty one.

"Excuse me Sir" I said, "Please don't go. It'll be a waste of your whole evening and your hosts will be very upset".

"You mind your own bloody business!" was all I got for that suggestion.

"Look, Sir, if you take off your black bow tie and put on an ordinary one, it will seem that you've got a dark lounge suit on. I could lend you my tie ... "

"No. No" he said, "I don't want any tomfoolery like that".

He'd cooled down a bit however and as I looked at him I had another idea.

"Sir," I suggested, "You're about the same height and build as I am, perhaps broader (cunning Ben!) I've just changed out of my brand new suit. It's in a case in the Ladies' Room just there, which no one will be using this evening. There's privacy, mirrors, the lot there for you. Try my suit, Sir." "No" he said.

"Please, Sir" I pleaded. (some more guests were in sight and I'd have to start announcing in a few seconds).

"Where is this blasted case, then?"

"Up those stairs" I breathed – and he vanished, in time for me to start announcing the next batch of guests.

Some hundred and twenty further guests arrived in the next fifteen minutes including the dour, correct, and unsmiling Russians. I was kept so fully occupied with them that the earlier incidents of the evening passed completely from my mind.

Another guest appeared at my elbow; a nice, broadly smiling, very pleasant gentleman. Somehow he looked familiar; his tie almost spoke to me – and it nearly said, "Society of London Toastmasters!! My tie; and my suit! It was old NASTY; he looked magnificent and he was tickled pink.

I announced him in my grandest voice and he chortled up to the President – the perfect guest.

During dinner he was the life and soul of his end of the table and after dinner he introduced me to at least five difference parties as "the gentleman who owned the suit." Obviously it had been a great talking point during the evening.

It was a happy incident (even though I had to wait an extra three quarters of an hour to get my suit back) and it was beautifully rounded off the <u>next afternoon</u> by the arrival at my home of a very large bottle of whisky and a nice letter from one of Britain's biggest ship-owners.

---

49. Follow the experts

In twenty years of Toast-mastering I must have given 'The President's/Master's permission to smoke' after the Loyal Toast, some thousands of times.

The announcement is always greeted with a muffled cheer, the rustle of hundreds of packets of cigarettes, the scraping of matches against match-boxes and the appearance of puffs of smoke above the tables. It's quite a moment.

I've got so used to it that if there is any variation I react like the man in the house nearest the Coastguards' fog-cannon at a Newfoundland seaport. (You will remember they fired the cannon every fifth minute for twenty years and once, when they missed a firing, he dashed out crying 'What was that?'.)

Recently, at a Dinner at the Royal College of Surgeons for the International Society of Oncologists, I duly gave the normal, 'President's permission to smoke' and was casually resuming a conversation with the Head Waiter when we both suddenly felt aware that something was wrong … no noise, no smoke.

'You told 'em, didn't you?" he asked.

'I did, didn't I?' I replied. And then, as if to prove I had, two people lit up; but only two – out of four hundred.

I asked the Head Waiter just what Oncologists did for a living. He said he thought they collected sea-shells(!) but later I learned that they are the world's greatest experts, researchers, writers and lecturers on, and the busiest examiners and cutters-out of, CANCER.

I thought it most significant.

50. A nice little incident

I once had occasion to take a wristwatch for repair to the tiny Mayfair office of an American electronics firm and while waiting at the counter for its return, heard a familiar and friendly voice call from the front doorway, "Excuse me folks. Is this Fairchild's?"

"Yes it is, Mr. Pete Murray" I smiled (for it was the famous broadcaster) "come this way Sir".

As he approached the counter with a courteous "Thank you" he flashed me a second glance and murmured "I seem to know your face and voice but can't remember from where".

"That's the story of my life, Sir" I laughed. "A known unknown. I'm a Toastmaster and I announced your speech at a Luncheon last week".

"Of course!" he said, "And what a nice, warm-hearted party that was."

"It really was, Sir" I agreed, "but the one you're coming to next Wednesday will be just as nice in its own, starchier, way".

He looked puzzled so I continued, "The Lord Mayor's Banquet for Arts and Learning, I saw the Guest List this morning – you're under 'Arts' and they've even remembered to show your new O.B.E.".

"My goodness, that's right" he gasped "and this is fate. I've been worried about that Banquet. The Invitation Card says 'Decorations to be worn' and I've not actually got my gong yet. You're probably just the man to tell me. Must I wear a miniature? And where the hell can I get one?".

"Well I think you should wear your O.B.E., Sir, as it's listed, and you can get a miniature either in the shop at the Piccadilly side of Golden Square or in a place down the hill from Moss Bros, on the left as you go towards the Strand."

"Great!" he said. "Do you happen to know the names of the shops?"

"I'm afraid I don't, Sir" I replied, "it's just that I remember looking in the windows as I've walked past".

"Damn" he muttered, "I might have been able to 'phone them … I can't go round there as I am on the way up North and won't be back until Tuesday".

"Well, I'll be walking through Golden Square in about half-an-hour's time" I mused "can I look in for you, and 'phone details to you somewhere?"

"No, not all the way to Scotland, old boy" said Pete, "forget-it. But thanks very much for the thought".

"What about if I can buy one for you and have it ready for you on the night?"

"Would you?" he smiled, "That would be marvellous – can I give you some money now?"

"Leave it to the night, Sir, in case I can't fix it".

So off I went to Golden Square only to find that the shop had gone out of business! Determined, however, to help this very likeable man I carried on to the shop near Moss Bros. – only to find that it had no O.B.E's !

"Can you get one made up?" I asked the middle-aged shop assistant.

"Takes about a fortnight, Sir" he said.

"Can you get one by next Tuesday?" I pleaded, "It's something special" and told him the story.

"For Pete Murray, eh?" he pondered "I <u>like</u> him. I'll see what I can do…"

He must have liked Pete a lot because the miniature was ready in two days. "Tell Pete we pulled out all the stops for him and we'd like an autograph for the shop!"

"You'll get one" I promised.

Thus it came to pass that, on arrival at Mansion House the following Wednesday Mr. Pete Murray was "nabbed" in the cloakroom by two members of the Security Staff and escorted to the Sheriff's changing room. There, before an interested and hurriedly assembled little knot of attendants and wine waiters, he was ceremoniously invested with his medal by Nick, the Lord Mayor's Yeoman who, amid polite applause performed the pinning-on presentation in the manner he'd observed during his service with the Scots Guards!

Only then was Pete allowed upstairs to join the line of famous entertainers, artists, authors and dons waiting to be announced to the Lord Mayor and as he approached the Announcer, instead of giving his name, he whispered, "I'm gonna 'do' you!" to which I solemnly replied "Thank you Sir" and, turning to the Lord Mayor (who was aware of his Yeoman's extra duty that day) proclaimed "Mr. Pete Murray – An Officer of the Most Excellent Order of the British Empire!"

I met Pete after the Banquet and found him very tickled by the whole affair. It wasn't quite Buckingham Palace, he felt, and Nick, at six-foot-four, in no way resembled the Queen …but the memory would stay with him for a long, long time.

He paid me there and then and, on my request for an autograph for his helpful fan in the medal shop, provided a glowingly sincere note which the man was proud to show to his customers.

A nice little incident. I like life when it's like that – with people getting a lot of fun by just trying to be nice to each other, and being appreciated.

51. Short front and backsides

Waiting apprehensively in hospital for an embarrassing and painful operation on my rear I suddenly became aware of a wizened old man peering very short-sightedly toward the name plate at the end of my bed.

"You Sullivan?" he croaked.

"Yes, that's me" I replied, "what can I do for you?"

"Ar gotta shive yer" he said.

Although surprised at the idea of such deluxe service on the N.H.S., I nevertheless had to decline …"Sorry, chum, I shaved myself only half-an-hour ago".

"Nah" he countered, "not your face – dahn below. All the hairs a gotta go – cawse they 'old bacteria".

The penny dropped and so, as he laboriously pulled the curtains round the bed, I removed my pyjama trousers; and knowing the exact site of the operation, turned face downwards on the bed.

"'Old on mate" he cried, "I always do the front first".

The front! Fear began to grip me. That was a very sensitive area with some extremely awkward angles and curves – to say nothing of a half dozen tiny warts. But it had to be done and I turned, shivering a little, on to my back and opened my legs. He seemed in no hurry, however, and I watched fascinated and appalled, as he opened a battered old tobacco tin and, with quivering hands, carefully selected one of several rusty razor blades.

Then, using no lather, he set about his task. I tried to relax with the thought "He's done this hundreds of times" only to remind myself, "He couldn't even see the large name plate above the bed!"

Eventually, with lots of holding of breath, stiffening and writhing on my part the front was done and, minus one groin wart, I was able to flop back on my pillow, exhausted.

The old chap was kindness itself. "Ave a little blow, mate" he murmured, "an, when you're ready, I'll 'elp you turn over".

Gratefully I agreed and rested for a couple of minutes whilst he changed blades.

"'Ere we go mate" he called, comfortingly, and came to lift me by the shoulders.

It was only then that I was able to read his hospital name-badge. It proudly said "HAIRDRESSER".

52. A bone in the throat

One night at the Europa Hotel enjoying my second course, which was trout, I suddenly realised that I had a bone stuck in my throat – a horrible feeling. The usual precautions of coughing, eating hard bits of bread, wouldn't move it and I began to get worried. The guests were getting to the end of the course and I realised that to be in a fit condition to introduce the speakers at the coffee stage I would have to remove the bone quickly.

I went to look into the cloak-room mirror and reached down for the bone with my finger but this made me feel bad. The cloak-room attendant, a Polish chap with a longer (but dirtier) finger also tried, but only succeeded in making me feel worse. He made a good suggestion however. "Why don't you get a taxi and go round to St. George's Hospital. They'll get it out with a pair of tweezers".

I looked in at the guests; they were just starting their main course, which would last half an hour and they would then have the sweet course, which would take another quarter of an hour. Thus I had forty-five minutes before my next announcement which was to be the Loyal Toast. I made a quick decision, put a raincoat over my red-coat and dashed out. Luckily there was a taxi which had just deposited someone at the hotel. "St. Georges Hospital, quick" I croaked.

Within a few minutes we were there. I paid the taxi driver far too much and he was off.

Dashing in I had to face the inevitable form signing. "Can't it be done without the forms?" I pleaded. "No" said the Receptionist, "We must complete them in case you die on us".

Ultimately I found myself in a small queue of people, all needing some form of out-patient treatment. They gave me rather interested glances. It was a bit unusual I suppose seeing a chap with a bright red-coat and full evening dress showing under his raincoat.

"Folks" I squeaked, "I wonder if you'll allow me to jump the queue a bit. I'm a Toastmaster at a banquet and I've got a bone stuck in my throat. It will have to come out before I can announce the speakers and I've got to get back in about ten minutes".

They all agreed and I took my place at the head of the queue next to a lady with a smashed nose and two deep black eyes. Very bad black eyes. "What's wrong with you dear, been in a car accident?" I asked. "No" she said, miserably, "My old man's just done me up". It was staggering. How could a chap do this to his wife? If I even speak roughly to mine it worries me for hours (in case she wallops me one).

I said as gently as I could. "You go first dear", but she replied, "That's alright mate, I'm in no hurry, I don't want to go home".

It's a forever memory for me, the way that poor woman just sat there after some bully of a husband had smashed her full tilt in the face.

Anyway, into the doctor I went. He took one look and said, "Oh, there's a bone there". "Yes" I said patiently "Can you get it out?" "Hold on a minute" he said putting a metal object in my mouth. Then, "Damn, I've missed it. Anyway it's out. It fell inwards but it won't hurt you". I felt better immediately and with a quick, "Thanks Doc" to the medic, a "Good luck" to the battered wife and my other new friends and I was off, to mild cheering.

Another hectic and expensive taxi-ride and I was back at the Europa, just in time to see the waitresses clearing the sweet plates and putting the coffee cups on the table. In other words, just in time to call upon the Chairman to propose the Loyal Toast. No one noticed my panting and I don't suppose any of the guests had an inkling of the great drama played out whilst they were eating.

53. Miss Page

As I think I've said before, people are always surprising.

Once your speakers at a banquet get to their feet and start giving a speech they are on their own and you have to leave it to their judgement.

One evening, having called upon a Mr. Page to propose a toast to 'The Ladies' I then had to call upon a Miss Page (no relation) to respond on their behalf.

She, a very demure little thing, opened by commenting on the fact that she had the same surname as the previous speaker and wondering if he and her audience knew of its origin.

'Apparently' she explained, 'if one of the monarch's mistresses produced a child, the king took responsibility for it, brought it up as a member of the Court and gave it the surname Page.'

'So Mr. Page,' she continued, 'as one bastard to another, thank you for your Toast.'

54. Muslims as well now

One of a Toastmaster's duties at a wedding reception is to announce the names of the guests, so that the Receiving Line (Bride's parents, Groom's parents, Bride and Groom) can get to know their new in-laws and friends.

Naturally, there will be many guests with the same surname as the Bride or the Groom; thus at the wedding of a Miss Smith to a Mr Brown there might be ten "Mr and Mrs Smiths" (her relations) and as many "Mr and Mrs Browns" (his relations).

At the arrival of the third pair of Smiths an experienced Toastmaster will probably say, "Lots of Smiths here today, Sir. May I have your Christian name?" and will announce, "Mr and Mrs John Smith", "Mr and Mrs Charlie Smith" and so on.

At one of my weddings, when the Cohens were marrying the Goldsteins, I put the question to the third Mr Cohen.

With shoulders shrugged up to his ears, arms held out, palms upward, and a pained expression on his face, he gasped, "My Christian name?"

Since that moment I've tried to remember, at Jewish weddings to ask ... "May I have your *First* name, Sir?"

55. Upstairs, downstairs

I was once given an engagement at one of our greatest hotels for the 'Blank and District J.P.A. Banquet and Ball' and imagined that it would be in connection with a Justices of the Peace Association.

I recall being a little disappointed on arrival, to find that it was in fact for the 'Blank and District Joint Palestine Appeal', i.e. a Jewish function rather than a legal one and therefore with a much less disciplined assembly which would be more difficult to control. (I like and admire Jewish people but they don't stick to convention – which is tough on Toastmasters).

A fine dinner was served followed by an appeal for Jewish refugees made by the Israeli Chief of Staff, who was en-route to take up his appointment as Israeli Ambassador to the U.S.A.

His name was Yitzhak Rabin and he gave the most statesmanlike speech I've ever heard; I was sure he would have an even greater future and I'm pleased to find that this brilliant soldier (he planned the six day war) and humanist (he wanted to help both Arab and Jew) was later the Prime Minister of Israel.

Then came the collection. During the appeal a printed card had been handed round to each of the guests who (knowing their duty) had entered thereon their name and the amount they would contribute. The cards were collected and the lady secretary brought them up to the top table where a young Jewish dynamo, who now controls a vast entertainment and gaming enterprise, had taken over the microphone.

"I've got the first card", he said, "dear old MOSHIE … (Chairman of a big tobacco company) has given his usual £8,000. Thank you Moshie …"

"And the second card. Thank you Mr… (a well known lawyer) for a very generous £5,000".

This continued, with the occasional, less enthusiastic, "And £25 from dear Mrs … who we know, gives all she can afford", until all cards had been collected and read. The Dynamo then asked the Treasurer, who'd been totting everything up, what the total was and, on being informed 'about £32,000', announced, "We're still below last year's record which I'm determined to beat. Will anyone offer more, please?"

"Make my three hundred pounds into three hundred guineas", called one lady. "The extra can be on behalf of my grandchildren".

"That's more like it," said Dynamo. "Now what about some more? Let's beat that record." There were no more offers however and, although it was no business of mine, I began to feel a little embarrassed. These people had good-heartedly given large sums of money and it seemed a little infra dig to squeeze for more. Enough was enough, surely.

Not for Dynamo, however.

"I'll tell you what" he said, "I'll instruct the Treasurer to change all the contributions from pounds to guineas. That'll bring us over the record figure. Any objections?"

Surprisingly, there were none and the new record was established. Dynamo had done his job.

I remember feeling quite angry that everyone so calmly accepted this further spending of their money when they'd already been so generous, but as a servant onlooker I could of course only stand silently and wait for a signal to make the next announcement. This, I had been forewarned, would be to advise the guests of a short break before the opening of the Ball. Before the signal could be given, however, there was a sudden and dramatic interruption by an elderly gentleman in the body of the hall.

"Mr Chairman", he cried, "my brother and I wish to donate £66,000". Sensation. Pandemonium. A standing ovation and the Dynamo almost crying into the microphone; even the wine waiters came back to see what had happened.

When things quietened a bit, I got my signal to announce the break and said something like "There will now be a short interval before the dancing to enable you to visit … your friends at the other tables."

The guests, who had been sitting for some two hours, accepted the implied advice gratefully – and moved with dignified haste towards the doors.

It was thus that, some ten minutes later, I found myself in the Gentlemen's room standing next to the chap who had made the Grand Gesture. He made to leave before me but was checked by the smiling courteous attendant who insisted on brushing some imaginary crumbs from his suit.

Snorting slightly, the guest searched for a coin (at which the smile, courtesy and brushing had all been directed) pressed it into the attendant's hand and moved on quickly.

Spotting a fellow worker in whom he assumed he could confide, the attendant showed me the coin and hissed, "See that, a tanner, in a posh hotel like this. The mingy bleeder".

"He's not really," I said. "He's just given away £66,000 upstairs".

56. A small favour

Some of my Toastmastering memories are not from Toastmastering at all but from the journey home after an engagement – like the time my wife and I were driving southwards down the Old Kent Road just after one o'clock one cold winter's morning.

"Rosie" I suddenly called, "I think that girl up the road there is in some sort of trouble – see if she's alright, will you ? If I call out I'll probably frighten her."

I then eased the car into the pavement where I'd seen a young woman half-running half-stumbling along.

My wife, by now well used to my sudden, intuitive observations, wound down her window and as we drew level with the girl called out in her soft and very kind voice "Are you alright dear? Can we help?"

The girl hesitated for a moment and then turned. She was sobbing, broken-heartedly but was able to gasp "Arve jus bin told me Dad's bin taken to 'ospittle – an 'ees dyin – an I won't be able to get there in time."

"Whereabouts is he, dear ?" I called from the driver's seat.

A further anguished moan and she sobbed, "I dunno, Mum's phoned me and me sisters and we've all gotta meet 'er at New Cross – then share a taxi to the 'ospittle, but I'll never get to them in time, they won't wait too long."

"Get in – quick" we chorused "we'll try to catch 'em."

My wife helped the poor girl into the car and we shot off at high speed, racing against time down the almost deserted road and looking far ahead for a group of distressed strangers.

Towards New Cross Gate I spotted them half-a-mile up the road on our side and called "Could that be your family up there?"

"Oooh! I think so" she cried excitedly, so we sped on, hoping desperately that we'd found them.

Suddenly we noticed that a taxi on the opposite side of the road to the group was making a U-turn.

"They must have hailed that taxi" screamed my wife "Get there before they go off."

I thought about sounding my horn but then decided it might not be wise to draw attention to a car doing about twice the speed limit. Instead, I really stepped on the gas and was able to reach the taxi and block it, Z Car style, just as the last of the passengers got on board.

Apologising to the startled cabbie, we helped the girl from the car and as she climbed into the taxi, amid cries of "urry up Joycee" from the family inside, she turned and gave us a look we shall never, ever, forget.

"I will see my Dad nah" she said, firmly. "God bless the both of yer."

A great reward for a small favour …

57. Really wicked

One of the great trade fairs in London is operated solely by a man and wife team. It lasts about a week and then they spend the following fifty one weeks preparing for the next Fair.

Half way through the year they organise a lush Banquet and Ball for all their exhibitors. They wine and dine them with the maximum of expense but the minimum of formality and usually contrive to surprise them in some way or other.

One year the surprise took the (very nice) shape of the great international entertainer Eartha Kitt – "The wickedest woman in the world". Only our Hosts, the band-leader and I knew about this. I was only brought into the secret when the band-leader asked me to wait for half an hour after the dinner to ensure that the star remained outside the Ballroom until he was ready to present her; also that on cue she would make her entry through the proper door.

I was only too pleased to agree to this knowing it would be a thrill to meet such a world famous and unusual personality.

My wife had arrived to take me home and I suggested she wait with me near the door, pen and paper in hand, ready to ask Eartha for her autograph. We were joined there by perhaps ten hotel guests who seemed to have scented that a famous person was about to appear.

Suddenly, she was in sight. An excited whisper ran round the group as the hotel manager lead her over to us. He introduced her and I asked her if she would kindly wait a few moments while I warned the band-leader that she was ready. She agreed, most pleasantly …

I then introduced my wife, a sweet and chubby little housewife from Petts Wood, who shyly said, "May I have your autograph, please?"

The star's reply was astounding! "No. No. No! You can't. I won't give it! No. No." she screamed in a voice that made the chandeliers rattle.

We were all absolutely dumbfounded. Mouths dropped open, eyes popped and my poor wife's lower lip trembled …

Before we could draw breath, however, Eartha burst into great peals of laughter, grabbed my wife and smothered her with kisses. "I'm sorry", she said "I _am_ wicked, aren't I" – She then gave autographs to the now excited and laughing group.

I peeped through the door. The band-leader was just getting the dancers seated, "…ready for a surprise item." He noticed my bright red coat immediately and signalled that he would announce in three minutes. I beckoned to Eartha and she came to the door, bringing my wife and the rest of her "new friends", as she called them.

"About two minutes, Eartha" I whispered. "When he makes the announcement, the searchlights will swing to this door, I'll swing it inwards – and then they're all yours!"

"Thank you" she said, then added, "I feel so nervous, I think I might faint. D'you mind if I have a few puffs of your cigarette?" (With this she took a cigarette from my wife's hand and started to smoke it in a very agitated manner). "Why am I so silly, being nervous like this after all these years. I can't go on. They'll _have_ to do without me. You go on for me" (This to my wife whose lip started trembling again). "Please – you go on; I know you can do it …"

From inside, there was a roll of drums and a crash on cymbals. "Ladies and Gentlemen" came the band-leader's voice over the microphone, "wonderful surprise for you this evening. Specially flown here from Bermuda for this one engagement, ("I just can't go on" said Eartha) just for you ... that world famous star... ("You <u>will</u> take my place, won't you?") EARTHA KITT." The searchlights stabbed on to our door, I swung it open – AND EARTHA KITT PUSHED MY WIFE IN!

The looks on the faces of the audience were quite remarkable, but the look of terror on my wife's face will haunt me for ever.

Eartha then went in grinning wickedly, gave my terrified wife another kiss, and proceeded to give the stunned and bewildered audience an hour of superb entertainment.

Some gal!

58. No smoke without fire

It is very difficult to get people back on to a dance floor in large numbers after a break for cabaret or refreshments. One trick I used to employ was to announce that the next dance would be a Ladies' Invitation Waltz.

Waving the table plan, I would explain to the audience that during the dance the music would stop and a member of the orchestra would select from the plan the name of one gentleman. The lady who had invited that gentleman to dance would then receive, "one of our magnificent spot prizes".

This crafty move usually brought the crowd back in droves, at the cost of only one spot prize; it also brought the band-leader into closer contact with the dancers, which is always a good thing. When the music stopped he would run through the plan with a flourish, select a name and call it across the band to me to repeat over the microphone, "the lady dancing with Mr Charlie Brown gets a lovely prize". She would rush up collect her prize and I would then say, "carry on dancing please. Another name in a few minutes".

The next time the music stopped, my announcement over the microphone was "stay where you are please, Ladies and Gentlemen, whilst we ask the band leader to select another gentleman's name from the table plan".

On hearing the second name I would call, "the lady dancing with Mr Danny Smith" and wait for her to dash excitedly towards the band stand. When she got near however, I would whisper (but over the microphone) "sorry, Madam, there is no prize – its just that we've been asked to <u>warn you to be very – very – careful</u>."

This used to work like a charm and raised some great laughs. It was different from the normal 'three paces forward', 'three paces back' type of spot gag.

One Friday evening at a rather posh 'firm's do' at the Dorchester, I worked this gag and can well remember the band-leader flicking over the rather small sheets of an alphabetical list, keeping us in mock suspense for the second name and finally reading from the very last sheet, "Mr Weeks".

As usual I then called up the lady dancing with Mr Weeks and sprang the 'warning' on her. The gag went down as well as ever with a big laugh.

The following <u>Thursday</u> whilst I was in the office wrestling with an exchange control problem, one of the signatories who shared the room with me answered the 'phone which was serving both of us.

"Ben" he said, "you'd better answer this. Somebody wants to talk to you, personally, and he sounds a bit het up".

I picked up my extension to be greeted by "This is Weeks here, now I demand you to tell me which of my staff told you to use my name!".

"Excuse me, Sir" I said trying desperately to think of an exchange control case involving a Mr Weeks, "Who are you? What are you talking about?"

"Look" he snapped, "you called my name out at a dance, didn't you?" Well, you've caused me a lot of trouble".

It took a bit of thinking from me and quite a bit of prodding from him before I could even identify which dance he meant. Then suddenly it clicked and I remembered clearly, "O.K. Sir", I comforted him "I remember. Now what's the bother?"

It all came out in a rush. As soon as he'd got back to his table after the spot gag his wife had demanded to know why any girl should be warned against him, why everyone had laughed so much, why this, why that... and she hadn't stopped.

An intense feeling of sympathy welled up in me for the poor devil. It was now SIX DAYS after the dance and she was obviously still having a go at him; so strongly that he'd found my Bank number from my wife (who normally refuses to let anyone bother me at work) so that he could resolve the matter. It was all my fault too...

"Mr Weeks" I said, "I'm terribly sorry about this. All I can do, is explain that it was mere chance that your name was called. Neither the band leader nor I knew any of the guests; he could have picked any name from any of the twenty six sheets and in fact he flicked through most of them before stopping at the W's. Honestly Sir, it couldn't have been a more random selection".

He took quite a bit of convincing but eventually the sheer truth of what I was saying got through to the defensive wall he'd built up during the week's siege.

"Thank you, Mr Sullivan", he mumbled "I'm sorry but I had to ring, you understand. Now I'll try to explain it to her ..."

Again I had this tremendous feeling of pity and I heard my voice say, "Shall I talk to her Sir?"

Like a drowning man clutching at straws he said, "Oh, would you, would you ...?"

As I put the 'phone down and took a deep breath I found all the other Signatories looking at me. "What the devil was all that about?" they demanded.

I explained and they erupted into laughter and jeers; when I told them I'd agreed to 'phone the lady in question they jeered even more and announced their intention of listening in!

Their later comments were more useful however; they all said "be careful, Ben, you don't know what's gone on before".

I'd been thinking that myself, so I was careful. I 'phoned the lady determined not to do anything which might further divide this unfortunate couple, both of whom were complete strangers to me.

"Has he put you up to this?" was her snarled opening, as soon as I'd introduced myself. A good start I thought, but by patiently sticking to my true story I felt I was gradually getting through to her. Her comments became more reasonable ...

"Why did everyone laugh so much?"

"Where did you get his name?"

"There must have been a reason" etc.

"Well alright then", she concluded, after about five painful minutes, "let's leave it at that".

"Madam" I said, at last speaking firmly, "don't let's leave it at that. I'm a perfect stranger to you both, I've no reason to lie to, or for, either of you. I've told you the absolute truth. Now do you blasted well believe me or don't you?"

Strangely enough, this worked for after a short silence she replied, slowly, "Yes, I do".

I felt extremely relieved. "Well, when the poor chap gets home, give him a big kiss, eh?"

He later told me that she had.

Toastmastering is not all shouting, is it?

59. You've gotta get 'em ter luv yer

Taking over as the boxing M.C. at the Royal Albert Hall and Wembley in the place of a very experienced and well loved character, I encountered a fair amount of resentment from his old friends, the (very) rough and ready punters.

This was a set-back to my plans to bring a little more discipline to the proceedings because it was evident that, with these boys persuasion rather than coercion was advisable.

I realised I would have to bide my time in the hope that (like my wife) they would slowly learn to love me sufficiently to accept my guidance towards better behaviour.

I particularly wished to stop invasions of the ring, the unfair barracking of foreign champions and the throwing of bottles at the M.C.

My chance to be accepted came fairly quickly, as it happened, when announcing a minor bout between a jet black boxer from London and a blond white chap from Luton.

I routinely proclaimed, "My Lords, ladies and gentlemen. This is a middleweight contest of six rounds, three minutes each round – Presenting from Bethnal Green, <u>Charlie</u> Smith and from Luton, <u>Harry</u> Smith. At the weigh-in today, Charlie Smith weighed 11 stone, 6 pounds, Harry Smith 11 stone, 7 pounds. Your referee for this contest is Mr Harry Gibbs and your timekeeper Mr Jeff Williams".

I would then normally have left the ring, but some devil inside me prompted me to stay and to add "Charlie Smith" (pointing to the black man) and "Harry Smith" (pointing to the white man) "My Lords, ladies and gentlemen – THEY ARE NOT RELATED"

There was a sudden deathly silence (which had me worried) and then gales of laughter which rang round the great amphitheatre.

That lucky remark changed everything; I became "their boy" thereafter and they would do everything I asked. Then, through some crafty appeals (yes dear reader I'm crafty as well as loveable) I completely stopped invasions of the ring and the barracking of the foreign champions.

With regard to the bottle throwing everything was under control for many years until the riot at the Minter/Hagler world title fight, when I was hit in the back of the neck by a can of beer; but I forgave them when one chap explained, "Sorry mate, we was tryin to 'it Agler".

Stopping invasions of the ring was the proudest achievement of my career in the funny old world of Boxing and I wish my tactics had been copied by others in the foot-balling and cricketing fields; also perhaps by my successors – as I notice, from T.V., that ring invasions are again commonplace.

60. Getting the point

At the outbreak of the Second World War volunteers from Britain's Dominions and Colonies streamed in to join us. Australians, Canadians, Indians, South Africans, New Zealanders, Maltese, Bahamians, Newfoundlanders and so on…

It was most heartening and I was fortunate enough to join the Navy with the first draft of Newfoundlanders – actually entering Naval Barracks with them.

They were all fishermen. Simple, straight forward and tough men who knew all about the sea – but little, it seemed, about anything else. Today, they might be described as 'thick' but I think 'unsophisticated' would be a kinder and more accurate expression.

Anyway, I liked and admired them and shall always be grateful for the memories they gave me.

The first memory was born when some of us Cockneys joined the Newfoundlanders for a lesson about the Compass. The lecturer was a kindly old Chief Petty Officer pensioner recalled to the Service solely for the training of new boys, and with orders to break us in very gently.

"Sid – dahn lads" he said, "an look at this compass board. I'm gonna make you expert at it in one arternoon".

We listened attentively.

"Nah", he continued, "on a compass there are four Cardinal Points. NORF, SARF, EACE and WECE". And he pointed to each of them on the compass board.

We all nodded sagely.

"O.K?" he queried. "Well nah we'll go ter the 'arf-Cardinal Points – 'arfway between the Cardinal Points" – and indicating these with his finger, he slowly intoned:-

"NORF – EACE 'arfway between NORF and EACE"
"SARF – EACE – 'arfway between SARF and EACE"
"SARF – WECE – 'arfway between SARF and WECE"
"NORF – WECE – 'arfway between NORF and WECE".

He looked around, benignly, and said "Got it, lads?"

Surprisingly, it was the Cockney, landlubbers who nodded. The Newfoundland fishermen didn't seem too confident.

"Nair mind lads" comforted the nice old Chief, "it'll soon come. I'll teach you the old Navy way. We'll 'ave a go at 'Boxing the Compass.' It's a game. Like this … I touch one of the Points wiv me finger and say what it is; then, oo-ever I point to in the class 'as ter tell me the name of the opposite point. So, if I say "NORF", he calls out "SARF". Got it?"

More nods – and again I noted that the greater response was from the landlubbers.

"Right" said Chiefy, placing his right index finger on the word WEST and pointing to me with his left one, "WECE".

Concentrating hard and fighting a rising panic, I almost triumphantly called, "EACE".

"Good boy! GOOD BOY!" said Chiefy. "Well done, son". I felt proud.

"Nah" he continued, touching the word NORTH and pointing to a Newfoundlander, "NORF".

"WEST" answered the Newfoundlander.

"WECE?" said the Chief. "Steady, son. Fink again."

The Newfoundlander fort.

"EAST" he said.

"Nah, son", said the Chief, clearly shaken and actually tapping the word "SOUTH" on the compass board, "fink; fink."

"NORTH WEST" said the Newfoundlander.

"Si-lly bleeder" said a Cockney.

"Ere, 'old on", sighed our gentle Chiefy. "I've never seen anyfing like this before. Blimey, son, what sort of job was you doing before the kind Navy agreed ter look arter you?"

"I was a fisherman" came the reply.

The Chief nearly fell over. "A fisherman – and you don't know the bleeding compass?" He walked around a bit, definitely worried but calming himself admirably.

"But you must 'av used the compass every day on your fishing boat" he pleaded.

"No, we didn't carry one" said the fisherman.

"Owjer know which way you're going then?"

"Well, we never go out of sight of land".

"Cor blind ole Pete" gasped the Chief "no compass – never go art a sight a land. 'Ere wait a minute. What 'appens in fog? It's always foggy where you come from, 'orf the Newfoundland banks, 'Ow do you get 'ome then?"

The simple and true reply stunned the Chief and the Cockneys into silence.

"We smell and we listen" explained the fisherman. "The land and the fresh river water smell different from the sea and the land birds have different cries from the sea birds".

At least one Cockney kid learned a good lesson that day; and sometimes I think of that fisherman when I meet 'City' Cockneys who are expert with calculators and computers but can't recite their seven times table.

61. What's your job?

The second memory the Newfoundland fishermen gave me was when they joined us at Whale Island, the world's toughest gunnery school, to learn Naval Gun Drill …

We were to be taught the team-drill for the 'twelve-pounder', an anti-ship and anti-aircraft weapon, suitable for trawlers and other small ships, so called because it fired a shell weighing twelve pounds.

Having doubled all the way to the gun-battery (everything all day long was done at the double on Whale Island) we found that by some clerical error, the twelve-pounder gun was being used by another sweating and grunting team.

"Roight" says our Gunnery Instructor (a thin very nasty looking Petty Officer, who was reputed even to sleep in the 'Attention' position) "we'll show you the drill on a real gun – Double march."

The real gun turned out to be a six-inch gun of the type used on cruisers. It was about thirty feet long, took nine men to work it and fired a shell weighing about a hundredweight.

"Roight", said the Gunnery Instructor, "The first nine of you, get fell in, in front of the gun".

Still panting, and very apprehensive about the notorious and unsmiling monster in charge of us, we got 'fell in'.

"Roight" snapped the G.I., "I'm now gonna give each of yer a number and a job. You'll learn that job and then we'll keep changing round so that you learn all the other jobs. Got it?"

We all nodded obediently – too nervous to do anything else.

Pointing to each of us in turn, the G.I. began to chant an obviously well rehearsed spiel. "You're Number One – Gunlayer and Captain of the Gun".

"You're Number Two – Breechworker-in-charge-of-all-operations-in-the-rear-of-the-gun".

"You're Number Three – Trainer"

"You're Number Four – Loader"

"You're Number Five – Second Loader"

"You're Number Six – Clarkson case carrier"

"You're Number Seven – Cordite supply"

"You're Number Eight – Rammer" and

"You're Number Nine – Sight Setter and Commoonication Number".

Trying not to move our lips we kept murmuring our job description over and over again, terrified of being found wanting when the time came – as we knew it would.

"Roight! Now I'll show you yer positions at the gum. Number One – Gunlayer and Captain of the Gun – you stand 'ere.

Number Two – Breechworker, Charge-all-operations-in-rear-of-gun- you stand 'ere"… And so on, for the nine of us.

"Roight!" he barked. "You know your positions. Now, when I give the order "Gun's Crooo – Close up" you will, at the double, take your places – Gun's crooo – Close up".

Zip – and we were in position. So fast that I think we upset him – but he carried on bravely, full of evil intent.

"Roight! Now when I give the order 'Gun's crooo – Num-ber' you will, in turn, raise your right 'and and shout in a loud and seamanlike manner, your number and your job, Got it?"

"Gun's Crooo – Num-ber!"

"One" bellowed the first man, raising his right hand, "Gunlayer and Captain of the Gun!"

"Two!" yelled the second man – "Breech worker in charge of all operations in the rear of the gun". And so on. We got through and we got it right. Such was the power of fear.

"Roight. Now for the next step" said the G.I. (We could see the unpleasant anticipation in his eyes). "When I give the order 'CHANGE ROUND' you will, moving at the double, go to the position of the number above you. Number One becomes Number Two, Number Two becomes Number Three and so on and Number Nine becomes Number One – And don't make any mistakes".

"Gun's Crooo – Change Ro-und!"

Zip again – and we were in our new positions (Two of us bashed our heads on the gun-barrel but neither emitted the least sound).

"Gun's Crooo – Num-ber!"

Recovering well, the new Number One raised his right hand and roared "One-Gunlayer and Captain of the Gun".

A moment's hesitation and Number Two was able to cry, "Two – Breechworker-charger-operations-reara-gun".

Numbers Three, Four, Five, Six, Seven and Eight then did their stuff, in loud and seamanlike manner, but Number Nine a Newfoundlander who, as Number Eight, had had difficulty in remembering "Rammer", let us down …

"Nine" he gulped, "… Sight and Number".

The G.I. took a three foot leap through the air, in the 'Attention' position, landing nose to nose with the poor sailor.

"You're SIGHT SETTER AND COMMOONICATION NUMBER" he hissed, in his Portsmouth accent. "Ave you got-it?"

The quivering rating nodded.

"Roight! Gun's crooo – Num-ber!"

"One!" screamed Number One – Gunlayer and Captain Gun".

"Two!" – Breechworker-charge-operations-reara-gun".

"Three" – "Four" – "Five" – "Six" – "Seven" – "Eight" – and we all waited, flinching.

"Nine" it came, haltingly, "Setting Communion".

This time, absolutely quivering with rage and frustration, the G.I. screamed "SIGHT SETTER AND COMMOONICATION NUMBER, YOU DUMB CLUCK! You're in commoonication with the officer on the bridge through the earphones and he tells you what to set the sights at. Now, say it after me – SIGHT SETTER – AND – COMMOONICATION NUMBER!"

"SIGHT SETTER – AND – COMMOONICATION NUM-BER" said our hero unconsciously mimicking the G.I's Portsmouth accent.

"Say it again" insisted the G.I., "Five times".

"Sight setter and commoonication number

"Sight setter and commoonication number

"Sight setter and commoonication number

"Sight setter and commoonication number

"Sight setter and commoonication number

The G.I. gave a grunt of satisfaction and then with hands stiffly down the seams of his trousers and peaked cap set absolutely straight on his head, stalked right round the gun (this was like a walk round the average semi-detached house) passing close by each of us and causing us to blanch with terror.

Nearing the end of the circle he suddenly sprang at the Newfoundlander, pointing a rigid and nasty finger.

"WHAT'S YOUR JOB?" he screamed.

"I'm a fisherman, Sir" said Number-Nine.

62. The golden ball of Monaco

This Golden Emblem could be yours for 100 francs!

The magnificent emblem illustrated has been donated to Variety International by Cartiers of Paris for this convention.

It is made of solid gold and on the map are precious stones sited in territories where Variety tents function.

It is valued at 50,000 francs and is to be raffled among conventioneers, with all the proceeds going to International's Charities Committee for distribution to handicapped, orphaned and distressed children in all parts of the world.

Raffle tickets are 100 francs each and the draw will take place during the Convention.

Please buy as many tickets as possible, knowing that you will be helping our children's cause – and at the same time give yourself a chance of winning a wonderful gold emblem you will be proud to possess.

In the spring of 1977, I was fortunate enough to be invited by Variety Club International to officiate, with a colleague, at their six-day Convention in Monte Carlo.

For my colleague and myself it was a week of unparalleled splendour and excitement. We stayed at the fantastic Lloews Hotel, officiated at fabulous places like the Casino and the Sporting Club and mixed daily with famous beings like Prince Rainier and Princess Grace, Prince Philip, Prince Charles, the Aga Khan, Earl Mountbatten, Doctor Kissinger, Cary Grant, David Niven, Roger Moore, Sophia Loren, nine hundred other showbiz people and it seemed, half the world's photographic press.

Each of our Luncheon or Dinner engagements could provide an interesting story but let me tell you here of the Wednesday Dinner.

The highlight of that evening was to be the draw, by Sophia Loren, for the Golden Ball of Monaco. This 'ball' was in fact a globe of the world, made of gold into which were set diamonds and rubies, one for each city in which the Variety Club operated. It was held in the golden hand of a child – depicting the work done for the sick children of the world by the Club – who raise about three million pounds each year for the purpose.

The Golden Ball was valued at about £8,000 and the tickets were sold during the Dinner for about £12.50 each. Such was the mood of the evening that individual purchases of ten tickets were not uncommon and a few guests even bought a hundred tickets each. Quite remarkable when you think that they did this sort of thing every night of the Convention – after paying £1,000 per head just to attend it.

When the great moment came for the draw, Prince Philip called upon Sophia Loren to join him on the stage. Danny (my colleague) and I then escorted her from the body of the hall (or should I say, escorted that body from the hall?) and stood by as she mounted the steps. Unlike Princess Grace, she would never accept a proffered gloved hand to assist her in this.

She then drew the lucky ticket and passed it for me to announce the number. The winner, who became near-hysterical as his number was called, was an American theatrical agent who had bought a ticket in the name of his son – a very badly crippled veteran of the Vietnam War.

As the winner mounted the stage to approach Sophia, Danny carefully lifted the trophy from the pedestal on which it had been displayed and (as instructed) started to pass it to me, for me to hand to Sophia. Like every person in that great assembly, Danny thought that the golden hand and the golden ball were as one and saw no danger in slanting it as he came towards me. Suddenly, terrifyingly, the Golden Ball was in mid-air and only the Golden Hand was still in Danny's grasp.

Fear, like fame, is a spur and because my right hand was full of papers I made a frantic lunge at the ball with my left hand. I failed to grasp it but by luck pushed it upwards, amid further horrific screams and the £8,000 object d'art continued to float on air.

Danny, face ashen, tried to get his left hand under the thing (his right hand of course was holding the Golden Hand) but he succeeded only in deflecting it away from where I was making my second lunge – and the screams went higher.

Luckily, however, as Danny and I crashed into each other, the Ball was somehow between us, first at neck level and then after one last fright, at chest level.

We squeezed our chests together so tightly that there was a chance we might squash the Ball – but it was safe! (So was our future!).

We took the Ball and raised it high, and nine hundred people, led by Prince Philip, sighed with relief. Those sighs sounded like a Force 9 gale.

Then refixed in the Golden Hand, the Golden Ball was passed to Sophia. The worst moment of our lives was over.

Mike Frankovitch the Hollywood Producer later comforted me. "None of us knew it was in two parts" he said, "thank goodness you were so quick".

Then he added, with a sly grin, "… but you missed a great chance – you pushed it against the wrong chest!"

63. Gentlemen of the press

Mention of the world's Press Photographers recalls another incident with these gentlemen.

My final engagement in Monaco took place in the sumptuous Sporting Club, which is perched on the edge of a promontory there. About eleven hundred show-biz people had come, with the British and Monagesque Royals, to dine in honour of Doctor Henry Kissinger, to whom Prince Charles would present a Golden Heart of Variety.

A really great evening, as I recall, with a most magnificent orchestra and a finale during which the curtains on the bus-sized windows which overlooked the Mediterranean were opened electrically to reveal a golden shower of fireworks streaming <u>down</u> the outside of the glass.

Half-way through this wonder night I received a bizarre request/instruction from one the equerries. "Please take Princess Caroline to the lavatory."

I thought this a little strange; couldn't the royal nineteen year old take herself ?

Still, an order is an order, so I collected this very dishy damsel from the young Royals' table and proudly escorted her to the door of the Banqueting Hall, where the Chief of Police was waiting for us. He was about six foot seven tall, four feet wide and looked very nasty indeed. Caroline and I (!!) were to be glad of his company for the rest of our stroll for, as soon as I opened the door, we were besieged by a horde of pushing, shouting photographers, all fighting to get a shot of my charge. Flashlights popping all over the place, cameras clanking against each other (and rivals' heads!) and elbows going in everywhere. Very much like the boxing riots at Wembley, in fact.

The Police Chief who had had dealings with this mob several times during the week and therefore <u>really</u> hated them, made a path for us by the simple expedient of bashing through them. He was like a bulldozer with arms – and the foe went down like ninepins, their expensive cameras crashing to the floor with them.

The Princess and I followed and I was grateful for her protection over the next ten yards or so to the entrance to the luxurious Ladies' Powder Room.

At the door I stopped, as would any Gentleman of the Bank of England, and bowed as the Princess floated through; but the photographers all went through too, following her right to the door of her cubicle (letting her close it, thank goodness) and then waiting while she did what a gal had to do.

What a lot of absolute tripehounds!

64. Amazing Grace

During the seventies, I spent a busy but marvellous week in Monaco looking after Variety Club International and mixing closely with the likes of Prince Philip, Prince Charles, Princess Grace, Prince Ranier, Earl Mountbatten, Henry Kissinger, Cary Grant, Roger Moore, David Niven and Sophia Loren – to drop just a few names – Very nice too and more lively than working in Exchange Control.

At the time there was a lot of speculation in the newspapers about the purpose of Prince Charles' visit. Was he there to help Variety or to court Princess Grace's lovely daughter, Caroline?

This bait attracted press photographers from all over the world (including of course many from London) who hounded the young couple quite ruthlessly.

When Charles and Caroline weren't on outdoor engagements, the photographers would hang around outside the hotels where the Variety Club was holding its Luncheons or Dinners, hoping for the chance of pictures of the celebrities.

The gang were outside the lovely old Palace Hotel one afternoon when my colleague Danny, and I led Her Serene Highness Princess Grace out from a Luncheon-cum-Fashion Show.

Danny and I had worked out a slick routine for such occasions, whereby at the top of the hotel steps we would split, he going left and me right, then turning inwards, bowing as the Princess passed between us and giving the photographers a clear view of her.

On this occasion, just as we bowed, Terry Pincher, an ace photographer from a London paper, called softy, "Ben, your flies are undone".

I <u>knew</u> they weren't, but the thought of a revealing photograph in the "Standard" that evening with Princess Grace and perhaps a saucy caption, broke my nerve. So I made a lightning and (as I thought) surreptitious reconnaissance.

The whole of the Press Brigade thereupon howled with laughter. <u>And so did Princess Grace</u>.

---

65. A Tremendous Englishman

When on Monday 24th November 1975 the National Sporting Club honoured Graham Hill, the champion Motor Racer, it was I think one of the proudest and happiest nights of his life. Surrounded by true friends and admirers, including a member of the Royal Family, and enveloped in their warm affection he positively radiated happiness.

The evening absolutely bubbled along. Famous faces from all walks of life were present, enjoying the fine food and simply marvellous speeches. The last-but-one of these was a Toast to "Our Guest of Honour" and I've never seen men rise so whole-heartedly to drink a Toast as they did for that one.

Instead of straightaway calling upon Graham to respond, I then had to request the guests to move their chairs so that they could see screens at either end of the hall. Then the lights dimmed and we were treated to a film about the fabulous life of the man we were honouring, including his heroic, agonising rehabilitation and return to championship class after a terrible crash.

I found it very moving indeed – and there was the chap himself, within a few inches of me. Everybody must have felt the same way because, as the film closed there came a great

round of applause from the darkened hall, which erupted into cheers as a spotlight cut through the darkness to illuminate the living legend – Graham Hill.

It was then the turn of the Duke of Kent to present the Club's gift to Graham. He had said that he needed an executive brief case – so they'd obtained a rather swish one for him, with fittings made of gold.

Then it was Graham's turn. He made his speech from short notes which he'd written on his menu during the other speeches. It was brilliant and as I watched and listened admiringly from a distance of about two feet, I reflected that this chap had everything. He glowed with health and humour. He was handsome; unbelievably brave, very wealthy and famous throughout the world. He'd retired from his dangerous trade, thank God, before it killed him as it had so many of his friends and rivals, and he still had many years in which to use his undoubtedly great gift of communication to lead and inspire we lesser mortals.

His speech over, Graham received a heartfelt (as opposed to a dutiful) standing ovation. When eventually it died down, the President signalled me to ask the guests to stand, "To make way for the President, His Royal Highness, your Guest of Honour and your Principal Guests".

Carrying Graham's executive case I then lead the party through the cheering crowds towards the door. Reaching it and then bowing, I found that only the President, His Royal Highness and the other speakers had followed. No Graham.

Dashing back through the crowd to the top table I found the great man still sitting contentedly and smiling as he signed autograph after autograph.

With his extremely sharp sense of awareness he noticed me immediately. "Sorry" he said, "I should have come with you, but I can't let the boys down – and I'm really enjoying this".

"No bother" I replied, and meant it. "Here's your case, a souvenir ashtray and some spare menus. They'll be good memories".

He stood up and proffered his hand, which I was very proud to shake, and said, "that's very thoughtful of you, old chap – and thanks for your part in a wonderful evening".

Those were the last words he spoke to me. Five days later this tremendous Englishman was killed in a blazing aircraft. His brand new executive brief case with gold fittings, thrown clear in the crash was the only fully recognisable thing by which his identity could be established.

66. The rollicking barrow-boy

I spent three happy but tough years in the Chief Cashier's Office of the Bank of England and the post I enjoyed most there was the one dealing with bank-notes, their issue, use and misuse.

In most of the letters we drafted for signature by a chief, we would have to quote permission under (something like) "The Notes Act of 1872 and the Notes Act of 1925". This was necessary whether we were dealing with an application to use pictures of banknotes in an advertisement, an appeal for replacement of notes which had been damaged or burned or a plea from an organisation for the Blind that the Bank consult them before changing the size of banknotes.

The 'damaged note' applications were most fun. "Last night my husband came home from work and he threw his trousers on the table. The dog grabbed them and chewed them, including these notes" (The mind boggles).

Whatever the query however, it became second nature to say, fairly early in the reply, "permission under the Notes Act of 1872 and the Notes Act of 1925 is given/would not be given".

And what on earth has this to do with Toastmastering? Well … very early one morning as I was making my way home from a Banquet and Ball at the old Trocadero at Piccadilly Circus, I was accosted by a street vendor who held a large tea towel in front of me and said "e'yar, guv – a poun-note washin-up clawf, oh-nee one and six". It was a perfect replica of a pound note!

Dear reader, I'm sure I had my tongue in my cheek (but probably my Bank training had its effect!) because, in handing over the cash I said "Have you got permission from the Bank of England under the Notes Act 1872 and 1925, to sell these?

"Oh, …s", he said, "jer want one or don't yer?"

I bought one and later that day put it into the Chief's IN box with a note saying, "I purchased this at a quarter-to-one this morning from a barrow-boy in Leicester Square and when I cautioned him under the 1872 and 1925 Acts, he replied with one word, which I haven't heard since I left the Navy".

I received no acknowledgement or thanks for my dedication to the Bank's interests, but ten days later, whilst sitting at lunch with some other first class clerks, I was approached by the Principal of the Issue Office – then to us just about three ranks lower than God.

A very quietly spoken man, he whispered almost inaudibly into my ear, "And Sullivan, what was that word the chap said to you which you haven't heard since you left the Navy?"

I stood, respectfully, and said, quietly "…s, Sir" forgetting how clear even my whispers are.

"Oh!" he murmured and padded away, leaving me to finish my lunch basking in the admiration of my friends, none of whom had ever sworn at a Principal.

I still await the return of my tea-clawf".

<u>Editors Note</u>: Ben Sullivan never swears in front of women but is willing to disclose the offending word to any male reader who has difficulty in discerning it from his title.

Enquiries to Ben, please, on the back of a five pound note.

67. Robbie Burns knew something

When one of Britain's most creative advertising agents offered me the job of officiating at his daughter's 21st birthday party I accepted with alacrity, keen (as an 'ideas man' myself) to see what he would dream up for her great day.

The party was a huge success, mainly through the lovely little ideas (based on his daughter's job as a teacher) which our Host revealed as the evening unfolded. These were a continuing source of delight to the lucky girl, her guests and her Toastmaster – who like a comedian supplied with gags by a superb script-writer, enjoyed helping to put them over.

A few months later I received an invitation to look after the same beautiful young lady's wedding reception. She was marrying a handsome Polish/American Air Force Officer and his whole family (the Jablonskis) were coming over from the States; they'd never ever visited quaint Old England before; the reception was to be held in a fifteenth century hall; and so on … perfect ingredients for a lovely wedding. And so it was.

By now regarded as a family friend I was not surprised, two years later, to be asked to do the son's 21st birthday party. Another really great (and different) evening with football (the boy's passion) as its central theme and with visits from international soccer stars arranged and quietly paid for by thoughtful and inventive old Dad.

Finally came the party for the youngest child's 21st. This, explained Dad, would of necessity have to be a less exciting affair because she was a 'blue baby' and because he would this time have to invite more of the elderly Aunts and Uncles of their close-knit family.

It was to be held at the Savoy and in the River Room which, with its views over the romantically-lit Thames and tree-lined Embankment Gardens, must be one of the best sited rooms in London. Needless to say, I looked forward to it.

As soon as I arrived I was embraced by the Hostess and the birthday girl and (my usual luck!) kissed by grandma. A lovely welcome but where was Dad, and Mary the eldest daughter?

Dad they told me, was at a hastily arranged and vital meeting with his most important client. He had however taken his evening dress with him and had sworn that (no matter what the client thought) he would break away to be at the Savoy by 7.00 pm in time for the pre-dinner reception. Knowing Dad, I was sure he would do so!

With Mary, they explained sadly, it was impossible for her to come. She and her husband had moved to Albuquerque, New Mexico, 7,000 miles away and she could not get the time off from her job as a teacher.

This saddened me too, as Mary was a really lovely girl, full of fun. The show had to go on however and as soon as Dad, true to his promise had arrived on time I started to announce the guests. All greetings were very warm and sincere and almost every new arrival enquired after Mary, often venting such expressions as 'Well, it *is* a bit far to come for a party'; 'her job must come first'; 'it would be too expensive' and so on.

At almost twenty past seven I was about (from my hand-counter) to tell our Host that all his guests had arrived and that, if he agreed and the Chef and the Head Waiter were ready, I would announce 'Dinner is served' at the arranged time of 7.25 pm so as to get the guests seated by 7.30 pm.

He did agree and while the Head Waiter had the table candles lit, the Chef put the rather special main dish into the ovens so that it would be perfectly cooked by the time the soup and fish had been eaten.

At perhaps 7.24 pm Dad brushed past me saying 'don't announce dinner for a minute – I've got to pop into the Gents'.

Unusually, he *was* only a minute – re-appearing at the foot of the short stairway and signalling to me with a finger across his lips, to ensure my silence. Then he brought a lady into view, but kept her close to the wall so that her reflection could not be seen in the mirrored door of the River Room. It was Mary!

The sly old dog – he'd done it again! *That's* where he'd been all day. Meeting Mary and hiding her!

I was choked with emotion but still sufficiently professional to respond, when he whispered 'Announce her', to proclaim through the door, "MRS MARY JABLONSKI – FROM ALBA-KIRKEE!"

The result was sensational beyond the Host's dreams. Every woman in the room screamed with joy, burst into absolute floods of tears and rushed to embrace Mary and her parents.

Bang went any chance I'd had of announcing dinner on time and when some five minutes later I thought I might be able to do so there was another complication. Almost every one of the sixty ladies present had ruined her make-up and *en masse* (or should I say *en mascara?*) they moved off to the Powder Room for repairs.

Result? We sat down some twenty-five minutes later – by which time the candles were half-burned and the special main dish was well on the way to ruin. The Chef 'saved' it, of course, with much skill and gnashing of teeth, but it wasn't the masterpiece he'd planned.

The best laid plans…

68. One for the ladies

On the 12th April 1943 my friend "Kiwi" Twomey and I, two fairly new Sub-lieutenants in Combined Operations, delivered some two hundred happy-go-lucky sailors to the shore based H.M.S. "Sea Serpent", formerly known as The Bracklesham Bay Hotel and "Gibsons" and "Ideal" Holiday Camps.

While Kiwi went into the hotel to find out what we had to do with the men, I got them lined up in the roadway. He was back fairly soon with news that a senior officer would shortly be out to talk to the men before handing them over to a Chief Petty Officer who would log them in at one of the holiday camps.

We subbies, Kiwi said, would be billeted at the hotel itself and he was quite excited at the prospect. "Go and have a quick look, Ben," he ventured, "It's a smashing place!"

In the way of young men, perhaps, I countered with "Don't worry about the hotel – what's the Wrens like?"

"Well, actually there's one in there exactly the type you like" he laughed, "lovely fair complexion, beautiful blue eyes and slightly plump. Look through the window of the Reception Counter and she's under the clock. You've got to sign the Arrivals Book there, anyway."

I bounded up the steps, found the Reception, and while signing the Arrivals Book and looking at the clock to check the time (it was 11.03) I stole a quick glance at the Wren busily tapping away at the teleprinter on the desk below it.

Gosh! Kiwi was right this time. What a cracker!

Using my corny technique of tapping on the window and calling, "Yoo Hoo, Yoo Hoo." I managed to get Signals Wren Rosie Ross to turn and look towards me. I waved, and she smiled (sending my knees out of control) but I also sensed, correctly, that she was thinking "Not another one of those soppy subbies!"

==========

The 12th April 1968 was a Good Friday. I'd worked very late Toast mastering the night before and it was in fact my third very late night that week (in addition to very full day's work in Exchange Control) so I suggested to my wife that we had a good lie-in on Friday to recover. She readily agreed as, with three children, a Toastmaster, a dog, and a booking agency to look after, she needed a rest too.

At about 10.50 I got up to make the morning tea. While it was brewing I borrowed my younger son's large chocolate Easter Egg, opened it and placed inside a small felt-covered egg within which was housed a brooch in two shades of gold, depicting a lovely rose …

When all was ready, I took the tea tray up to the bedroom, complete with Easter Egg (calming my small son, who was by now getting tearfully worried about his egg) and at 11.02 had the wonderful experience of presenting it to my wife (calmly waiting for nothing more than another morning tea) together with the following poem, which she finished reading at precisely 11.03

AT FIRST SIGHT

T'was 11.03 I saw you, Rosie,
For the first time in my life,
I'm sure I knew – it's since proved true,
That you would be my wife.

T'was April 12th I found true wealth,
Lovely, smiling treasure.
And since that day, can truly say,
You've been my greatest pleasure.

T'was 43 we met, Rosie,
My heart grew a rose within it.
Dear little Wren, how I've loved you since then,
For twenty-five years – TO THIS MINUTE.

11.03 a.m.
Friday, April 12th 1968

Ben

Rosie, like 99.9% of the population had had absolutely no idea of the date and time we'd first set eyes on each other. She cried, I cried, our daughter cried and the boy (who thought by now that his egg had really gone for a Burton) cried as well. A really happy moment in all our lives – and good for a marriage.

After a success like that you can get a bit worried at what to do for the 35th, 40th, 45th Anniversaries but, by thinking and thinking, something can usually be managed.

Mr. Editor, if the ladies like this story, the gentlemen don't pull my leg too much and you give your permission, I'll cheerfully record the continuing stories of the Anniversaries of a real love match.

---

69. How to wet friends and influenza people

In 1943 the Russians, beleaguered by the all conquering German armies were calling desperately for a Second Front i.e., an invasion by their Western allies of some other part of the occupied territories like France, Belgium, Holland, Denmark or Norway – which would draw much of the Nazi armour away from the Eastern front and give the Russians some respite.

Sadly this call could not be answered until June 1944, but in early 1943 we chaps in Combined Operations were given the first of our Landing Craft and told to start practising the art of beaching, with soldiers of the Allied nations.

Among the first to be accorded this doubtful honour were soldiers of the Polish Brigade. I had a lot of respect and sympathy for these chaps. Driven out of their native land by the Germans and the Russians leaving their loved ones behind, they had fought their way to Britain so that they could continue the struggle with us.

To the Poles, practice in Landing Craft meant only one thing, the Second Front must be drawing near. It was a terrific morale booster for them and their enthusiasm knew no bounds. "Zoon ve vill be back int Poland" they rejoiced. "This iss vonderful!" And, keen as mustard, they listened to every word of my briefing.

"We shall turn in to the beach in a few minutes time" I explained. "As we get near I want you to crouch down so that you are protected by the steel doors. Keep your steel helmets on too, as some of my men, ashore, are going to throw stones at us, as though we were under fire."

On command they crouched down and I crouched with them whispering last minute instructions and whipping up even more enthusiasm. "We're approaching the beach now. Keep down. When we feel a slight jerk and hear a swish as we scrape into the sand, we'll slam open the doors and let the ramp crash down. You'll then shoot off as fast as you can and charge up the beach."

Using a little psychology, I added "Last week the Czech soldiers cleared the boat in 3 seconds; you Poles should be able to do it in two, I think."

"Ya! Ya!" they chorused, excitedly. Suddenly the jerk, the swish of boat against sand and they were off in about one second flat. I'd swear they went over the ramp as it was crashing down!

Perfect – but then they vanished from sight.

Instead of the beach, we'd come to rest on a tiny half-covered spit of sand some twenty yards from the shore. The Poles had hurtled out straight into about eight feet of freezing cold North Sea! And as they struggled to shore in their heavy gear over came the showers of stones from the "enemy" on the beach …

We collected them about ten minutes later, after they'd "captured" their objective on the beach, and couldn't fail to notice how water fountained from each of their boot-lace holes with each step they took; and how their clothes were thick with wet sand; how their teeth chattered; and how they looked enviously at us, warm and dry in our thick duffel coats…

I made a futile attempt to explain that there had been no spits of sand on our previous run and that it was probably caused by some peculiar combination of wind and tide … but there was no reply. In fact they didn't say another word all the way back to the base.

Shame really.

70. Lost leaders

Many years ago, soon after his victory in the Six Day War, I looked after Yitzhak Rabin during a Dinner at the Savoy. Listening to his speech I formed the firm opinion that here was a great soldier and statesman.

News of his recent assassination therefore really upset me; what a waste of a brilliant, humane man.

It also set me thinking of the assassinations of other of my world famous guests speakers like Earl Mountbatten with whom I spent nearly a week in Monaco (with Variety Club International) during which I had to organise photographs of Americans shaking hands with him at $1,000 a go (every dollar going to the Club's charity). And, when he found that I'd served under him (well under) in Combined Operations, he allowed a photograph to be taken of the two of us, for free.

Soon after, this great hero was blown to pieces off the north-west coast of Ireland by the IRA.

Then there was Sir Abubakar Tafawa Balewa, the Prime Minister of Nigeria. He came to London in 1966 to attend the Commonwealth Prime Ministers' Conference and gave a small Reception at the Nigerian High Commissioner's house in London.

I officiated as Toastmaster and my overwhelming memory of the occasion was the way I was restricted by his over-zealous, sinister looking bodyguards who, literally, wouldn't let me get within two yards of him.

I thought about this, three days later, when I read that, on his return to Nigeria, the Prime Minister had been kidnapped and killed and his body dumped on an ant-heap.

Some years later, in 1984, looking after an Indian businessmen's Banquet in honour of Mrs. Indra Gandhi, Prime Minister of India, at the Royal Garden Hotel in Kensington, I was somewhat shaken by the placards of a large group of protestors outside the hotel. Some said, "Murderer," others "Indra Gandhi – you killed my father."

Not a very nice welcome for a distinguished visitor!

Some months after this, having ordered her army to besiege the Sikh Golden Temple at Amristsar, she was assassinated by one of her own bodyguards – a Sikh who had been forced by his religious leaders to wreak revenge on their behalf.

Her son, Rajiv Gandhi, was then elected Prime Minister in her place. When he visited London in 1990 a State Banquet was given in his honour at the Mansion House. Again I officiated and, in my brief dealings with the great man, found him very charming.

Nevertheless, he too was assassinated some months later; blown to pieces, with his killer, a Kamikaze type young lady, who was presenting him with a bouquet which concealed a bomb.

I find that having met these world-figures, even briefly, news of their assassination really sends shivers down my spine. I sincerely hope that the other hundreds or so Heads of State I've looked after will be better protected.

71. Through bleary eyes

One engagement that sticks in my memory was in Geneva at the Hotel Intercontinental.

A very famous U.S. electronic organ company promised to give, to any distributor who increased sales by twenty per cent within a specified period, 'Seven days in Europe that you and your partner will never forget'.

Some three hundred and twenty distributors qualified and, with their partners, looked to the company to keep its promise. It did just that, filling two jumbo jets – one flying to Amsterdam, the other to Geneva. More about Geneva later, but at Amsterdam a chartered Rhine steamer awaited the 320 people who had flown there.

Once on board they were welcomed with an announcement: 'Ladies and Gentlemen, this is your ship: the bar opens at 10.00 a.m. today and closes at 4.00 a.m. tomorrow, re-opening at 10.00 a.m. and so on. Please, please, help yourselves. You've earned this'.

Then they, mainly U.S. citizens who (they told me) had genuinely never seen a building more than thirty years old, proceeded through ancient Holland, Belgium, France and Germany to Basle in Switzerland, being welcomed and feted, en route, at gorgeous romantic medieval castles.

At Basle they staggered from the ship, were poured happily into coaches and taken to Geneva to continue their holiday. On arrival there (as on their arrival everywhere) they were greeted with champagne and spent three more days enjoying the delights of Geneva, Montreux, Chamonix, Mont Blanc and so on and finishing with a Grand Banquet controlled by a REAL ENGLISH TOASTMASTER. (Please read that with an American accent!).

Those who flew to Geneva of course did the whole trip in reverse; three days in Geneva, Grand Banquet with Real English Toastmaster, off to Basle and on to the Floating Bar for Amsterdam.

The Real English Toastmaster, who hadn't sold an electronic (or even a mouth) organ in his life, was in the meantime doing rather well, joining the happy travellers on all their jaunts to concert halls, mountain tops, etc., and whispering the magic word 'Staff' on the few occasions when his un-American appearance aroused comment.

The cost of entertainment was staggering; in two concert halls, where we were entertained by world famous organists, two of the company's £16,000 organs, especially installed for the occasion were left 'With the company's compliments'. So were three other £5,000 organs which had been casually installed in the hotel for demonstration purposes.

The thing that really shook me however was when, midway through each of the Banquets, I was asked to announce: 'Ladies and Gentlemen – the President would like each lady to accept a small favour with the compliments of the Company'. This was a signal for his aides to present every lady with a £97 Jaeger le Coutre wristwatch! Brought up to regard 'pound a time' Ladies' Gifts as the norm at hundreds of Ladies' Festivals, I still vibrate slightly when recalling this £31,000 gesture.

I asked the organiser how long it would take the company to recoup the enormous costs of the Seven days in Europe. 'Sir', he said (showing all the usual American deference for Real English Toastmasters) 'it has all been met already, several times over, from the twenty per cent increase in sales'.

As I once said when handed £50 for an idea which saved the Bank in which I worked a few thousands a year: 'Incentives really do produce results!'

---

72. Pilkington man – or a bull in a trawler-ship

Danny Denahy

The frayed wire pierced my hand and jammed my thumb in the nozzle.

Serving on the small trawler H.M.S. "Ocean Brine" as a Leading Seaman in charge of Blue Watch (three A/Bs!) I had the doubtful pleasure of taking on board an Ordinary Seaman who was to replace one of my merry men. (I was 21, he and they were nineteen).

He joined us while we were on patrol, brought out from port by our "chummy" ship and he climbed on board like an old sailor.

He soon proved he wasn't however, when he slung his hammock in our Mess (the former fish hold) and used a slip knot to tie the ends – ensuring a slow but definite crash to the deck when he turned in!

Over the next few weeks he proved not only to be a most gifted singer of an endless list of popular lyrics but also the most awkward and accident-prone chap I'd ever met. This latter deficiency was important in a world of steam winches, heavy chains, lurching ships, sea-borne anti aircraft balloons, machine guns and so on, and it wasn't long before the rest of the Watch were refusing to work with "that awkward b...".

It was a situation which could not be allowed to continue ... three of us doing all the dirty work and the fourth doing nothing. He'd have to be trained, step by step, by a brave, patient, resolute and good-looking Leading Seaman. There was no contest, I got the job.

On Joe's second night we were as usual protecting England by lying at anchor off North Berwick and he and I were "Watch on deck".

Our duties, as I explained to him were to report the appearance of any other ship or aircraft, ringing the alarm bell if at all suspicious, and to watch that we weren't dragging the anchor. This last chore was a bit much for Joe, who couldn't quite get the idea of cross-bearings, but I didn't worry unduly as it was a very safe anchorage and we'd never dragged before.

An hour into the watch, alone with Joe whilst the rest of the crew stank and slept below, and having learned by heart one of his songs ("What is a Mummy, Daddy? Everyone's got one but me. Is she the lady who lives next door, washes the dishes and cleans up the floor" etc.) I introduced him to the tea ceremony.

This involved one man in the onerous duty of putting the kettle fully over the coal fire in the galley so that the much stewed water again started to boil, whilst the other chap went below to prepare two chipped enamel mugs, some condensed milk and oodles of sugar.

When the kettle boiled, the man on deck would bring it along to the hatch where the man below, hearing his mate's footsteps across the deck, would climb up the gangway ready to take the kettle from him, thus ensuring that the deck was always manned. He would then make the tea below, drink his own then go up on deck to let the other chap down for a while, in the warm.

This had worked perfectly with everyone else but Joe chose to turn into the hatch quickly and, as I came up the stairway, swing the kettle to me, spout downwards! I saw the boiling water cascading towards my face and jumped sideways taking it all on my shoulder – luckily protected by a thick duffel coat, a couple of sweaters and a flannel undershirt. My shout of rage fortunately woke the rest of the crew, who stopped me from doing young Joe some serious damage, but then they blamed me for persisting with the training of the silly so and so.

Danny Denahy

he'd attached the rope only to the lid . . . I ran

Persist I did, however, and when four days later, we entered harbour, I insisted on taking Joe with me to the Purser's Store and the NAAFI to get some stores. We got back to the ship with them and loading went well until, having lowered many articles to me by rope (I'd carefully taught him the requisite knots) Joe started to lower a large pot of grey paint. Calamitously he'd attached the rope only to the small handle on the lid and when, from my vantage point on deck, some thirty feet below, I saw the paint-pot appear with no rope around and under it, I ran. Just in time! Four gallons of paint crashed down on the deck exploding over about half the port side of our little ship, including the bridge and the funnel. Hanging from the quay was the tin lid and above it was Joe's puzzled face.

Foolish chap that I am, I grimly kept to my resolve of making Joe a competent member of the watch, able to do his fair share of the work and the next test came one blustery day when as we were entering harbour, I bravely made him help me wind down the anti-aircraft balloon which we carried to shield ourselves and our coastal convoys from diving enemy aircraft.

This was a fairly simple task; he just wound a handle round and round, turning it away from himself, then either just held it to stop the balloon from shooting up again, or let a metal bar down on to the cog wheels of the winding winch. This would act like a hand brake.

When the balloon was down to the top of the mast, and the balloon-boat had come alongside, a second man would climb the mast, taking with him a thin wire rope with a clip on its end which he would attach to a spare clip on the balloon's wire. When he'd done this, the bottom of his rope would be passed to the crew of the balloon boat who would pull the balloon down sufficiently to make our wire go slack. Our mast man could then disconnect our shackle from the balloon, which could then be taken away by the balloon boat.

On this occasion, because I'd noticed, when fixing the balloon for sea, that there was a fair amount of fraying where our wire was attached to the shackle, I told Joe that, after he'd wound down the balloon and I'd gone up and passed it over to the balloon boat, he should take the brake off and slowly unwind so that I could pull the wire through the revolving nozzle at the top of the mast and very carefully lower the shackle down to him at deck level. He would then hold it until I climbed down to repair it.

Care was needed in the lowering and holding because with the ship rolling madly, as trawlers do, the heavy shackle hanging on the end of a wire from the top of the mast would swing dangerously, pendulum fashion.

So … the balloon had gone and standing there on the thin ratlines at the soot-covered mast top, with the ship rolling about ten feet each side of true, I took a firm grip of the frayed wire with my soot-covered right hand and, pulling firmly on it, called through the thick clouds of black smoke which were now belching from the funnel, "Slacken off Joe".

His response to this was a quick turn of the winch-handle in the same direction as he'd been turning for the past half-hour! The opposite of slackening off!

The frayed wire pierced my hand in several places (mainly through that skin 'tween thumb and forefinger) and jammed the thumb – knuckle into the still half-revolving nozzle at the top of the mast.

Swaying up there, looking at the blood discharging from my trapped hand and oozing through the soot, I yelled, amid visions of lockjaw, "TUT, TUT, JOE, YOU SILLY BOY, SLACKEN IT!" (Or something like that).

He reacted very quickly – by taking another sharp turn on the winch handle. This time the frayed wired just pulled through and took away various bits of skin – but at least my hand was now free.

I really wanted to climb down and get in my bunk, or castrate Joe, or something, but we still had to get that blasted shackle down for repair.

"Joe" I roared "Lift the so and so bar and turn the handle the other so and so way!"

This time all went well; he slackened off and by pulling the wire through the nozzle I was able, very slowly, to get the shackle down to him. "Now hold it, and hold it tight you awkward git" I called, climbing down on to the rolling deck.

Joe then very obediently held the shackle while I cleaned my wounds with spit and hanky.

"Now, give me that so and so shackle" I growled.

Perhaps he didn't want to get too close to me, because instead of passing the shackle from his hand to mine, he swung it to me. I went to grab it. It careered to port with the roll of the ship. I turned. It came back on me splitting my upper lip and (as was later ascertained) slightly cracking a front tooth!

Perhaps the sight of the very wild looking, soot-covered, cursing monster in front of him, dripping blood from mouth and hand, frightened Joe, for he fled and locked himself in the paint locker!

I quickly forgave him, strangely enough. I'd seen a very scared little chap standing in front of me. And his balloon work definitely improved from that moment. Perhaps my small sacrifices were not completely in vain.

This 'teacherly' pride in making a chap that everyone else said was useless into a useful member of the team almost lead to my death later when I introduced Joe into the mysteries of the ship's steam winch, involving the winding, amid much clanking, hissing and billowing of steam, of the thick wires which held the ship to the quay or pulled in the very heavy minesweeping gear.

It is often the practice, as these heavy wires are winched in, for one deck hand to hold them taut so that they wind close round the winch barrel instead of billowing.

Having patiently taught Joe the winch work, I was holding the incoming wire fairly taut for him, letting it slip slowly through my hands, when, conscious that the badly frayed end was in sight, called "Slower, Slow-er Joe", as I had no wish for stiff, jagged, rusty wire to pass through my hands at speed.

Joe obediently and seemingly expertly slowed down by turning the steam control wheel towards himself ... "Slower ... Slower ... Slow-er" I called as the ragged mass entered my grasp "and STOP!"

At this Joe reverted to type and turned the steam control wheel to Full Power! The jagged ends of the great wire tore through my hands catching under my brand new 21st birthday ring and yanking me three yards forward hands and head first into the underside of the winch amid wires, hissing hot steam and great revolving steel drums!

Somehow I was alright after they'd cut the ring from my finger and dragged me out, and later that night as we all sat in the Mess Deck, my mates having fed me, as I couldn't manage knife and fork, the rough trawler man's talk good naturedly centred on Joe who, give him his due could take it well.

"Joe, yer silly sod" asked one of the boys "oo used to pay yer before the kind Navy agreed to look arter yer? Oo'd yer work for?"

"I was a porter at Pilkington's glass factory at St. Helens" came the astounding reply. " .. used to carry the glass about".

I couldn't laugh, with my steamed lips but the others went into fits ... "Did you ever 'ave an accident then?" cackled Taffy the cook.

In reply Joe took of his flannel (shirt) and displayed his bare back – with about a hundred small scars!

I parted company with him soon after that when I volunteered to serve in Assault Landing Craft (I thought they'd be safer) and have never seen, or heard of Joe since; he may not have survived the War.

I hope he did, because he was a nice character.

I doubt he went back to Pilkingtons as I understand they are still solvent (!) but perhaps Sir Alistair Pilkington could find out for us. Joe's surname was either Travers, from a village called Prescott, or Prescott, from a village called Travers, and he'd now be about sixty-eight.

73. All will be revealed

About twenty years ago, my wife Rosie and I were walking arm-in-arm in the shopping area of our little town, when, noticing something amid the paper litter in the gutter I said, "There's a ring down there" and made to pick it up.

"Leave it," laughed Rosie, "it's one of those new ring-pull things from the Coca Cola tins; they look like silver rings, side on."

Picking up the object and passing it to her I murmured something like, "Since when have they been fitting three-stone diamond rings on Cola tins?"

She grabbed it from me, astonished and worried. "What a shame! Some poor girl's lost her engagement ring", she lamented. "I'll bet she's pulled it off when she took off her glove; she'll be broken-hearted."

"Or perhaps she had a quarrel with her boy-friend and threw it out of a car window?" I suggested.

"Tell the police, Ben, she'll be worried out of her life now, whatever the cause."

As soon as we arrived home Rosie got me to telephone our local Police Station in Chislehurst and report the finding of a ring. "Anyone who describes it accurately can have it" I told them, defensively.

We heard nothing and, after a couple of days, Rosie insisted we called another "local" Station in St. Mary's Cray. Then the one at Bromley and finally the one in Orpington.

After a month we received a call from a lady in Southend who thought she might have lost her <u>solitaire</u> diamond ring while on a visit to our area and had rung the Orpington Police in desperation.

Finally, after about seven months, the Police informed me (as a finder) that, in the absence of any claim, the ring was mine.

Prompted by Rosie I told them that if the lady owner ever turned up it was still hers. Their response however was that, in their experience, claims after six months were completely unknown and they were taking the item off their books.

So I formally gave the ring to Rosie and, after a couple of years dithering, she accepted that it was actually hers and started to wear it.

Recently, after a very revealing session with a spiritual medium at the Spiritualist Association of Great Britain in Belgrave Square, Rosie thanked the lady and was making her way out through the doorway when the medium called, "Excuse me dear, could you come back a moment ... I'm getting a message ... from a lady."

She then said, "Do you ever wear a ring ...which was found by somebody else...and given to you?"

"Yes!" gasped Rosie, "This one. My husband found it about twenty years ago and gave it to me."

The medium then continued, "The lady says, "Thank you for all the efforts you made in trying to find me."

"You see dear" explained the medium "this lady has now passed over – and she says she wants you to wear the ring always and hopes it will bring you great happiness."

---

74. Drinks later

When Sir James Miller, a Scot who had been the Lord Provost of Edinburgh, achieved the unique distinction of also becoming Lord Mayor of London, he promised that during his mayoralty he would hold a Burns Night – with the Haggis, neaps and tatties and all.

This promise was fulfilled one famous evening at the City Livery Club on the Embankment. I was privileged to be the Toastmaster and, at the appropriate stage of the meal, went into the kitchen to form up the small procession of two Scottish pipers and the Chef who was to carry the Haggis. Then carefully explained to these gentlemen that I would immediately go back into the Banqueting Hall to ask the assembled guests to "Welcome the Haggis."

I stressed that, on the cue word "Haggis" the small procession should enter through the kitchen's OUT door (which was on the Lord Mayor's left) and with pipes a'playing, come up behind the Lord Mayor, where the Chef should "present the Haggis" first to him and then to the eminent Scottish poet who was to "address" it, before placing the "wee beastie" on the table in front of the latter. The procession should then retire by way of the IN door which was on the Lord Mayor's right.

I then made the "cue" announcement "Mr. President, My Lord Mayor, Aldermen, Sheriffs and Gentlemen – would you please welcome the Haggis" and swung my left hand theatrically to draw attention towards the open OUT door and the Grand Entry.

Nothing happened!

This is about the worst thing that can happen to a compere, of course, but I was among sympathetic friends and was able to give them a wan smile before striding grimly to the OUT door.

Poking my head in I hissed, "You missed it lads, so I'll do it again. Come in on the word 'Haggis' this time."

Then I made the announcement again. "Mr President, My Lord Mayor, Aldermen, Sheriffs and Gentlemen – would you please WELCOME THE HAGGIS!"

At this just one piper came in (with bagpipes but no music, no chef, no second piper and no haggis), staggered crablike along the back of the top table and then vanished through the IN door.

The faces of the eminent City men were a study!

I went back into the kitchen for a very earnest, heart-to-heart talk with my idiot friends and then tried it all over again.

This time, amid amused cheering, we got it right but there and then I vowed that in all future dealings with Scottish pipers I would do my best to ensure that the staff refrained from giving them their multiple wee drams of whisky until <u>after</u> they have finished their performance.

75. Grandma's being strangled

Vitners' Hall, home of the Worshipful Company of Vintners, is one of those charming old City of London livery halls which are jewels in the City's heritage. There has been a Hall on the site for some centuries and the present one is over three hundred years old. A place of great beauty and peace which, in its fine banqueting hall proudly exhibits a plaque listing five Kings who dined together at Vintners in 1363.

I've been Toastmaster at several lovely banquets there over the past thirty years, notably at one of the famous Swan Festivals, when to celebrate the annual marking of the Vintners and Dyers swans, the Company sits down to dine.

One banquet I missed, however, and truly wish I <u>had</u> been at was a certain "Burns Night" given by the Worshipful Company of Distillers.

Imagine the scene. One hundred and forty guests in full evening dress, or dress uniform; a horse-shoe table and one centre sprig set for a very expensive meal. Cutlery and glasses (five per guest) polished to perfection. Flowers at every yard along each table, already laden with candlesticks and gold and silver trophies. Behind the circular end of the horseshoe (which was in effect the top table) and set into the wall, was an alcove with shelves displaying punch-bowls, loving cups, and rose-water bowls. All made of silver and gleaming softly in the candlelight. Magical.

It was time for the presentation of the Haggis and, led by two Scottish soldiers playing their bagpipes, the Chef marched in from the kitchen carrying the "Wee Beastie" on a silver tray. He was to place this before the Master Distiller, who would then "address" it and then "stab" it.

The pipers approached the Master one from each side of the horseshoe, meeting behind him but standing back as far as they could, near to the alcove, leaving room for the Chef to step in and offer the Haggis to him.

The sound of two sets of bagpipes at full blast in a small hall is a bit of a trial for diners – even on a Burn's Night. It was far too much for "Mickey" the Hall's pet cat, sleeping, as was his wont, in one of the punch-bowls in the alcove.

He woke, with an absolutely blood-curdling scream (possibly thinking he'd heard a relative being strangled) and sprang from his silver bed straight to the shoulder of his nearest tormentor. That worthy Scottish warrior immediately sucked instead of blowing and Mickey jumped ever forward, over the Master's throne, landing with a crash of breaking glasses, on to the Top Table.

Kindly hands tried to stop the terrified pussy but by then, what with the excited cries of the guests and the agonising death rattles of the bagpipes as they were stopped, every sound or movement was a threat to the poor creature.

Like a small, hairy, jet propelled bull-dozer he shot down the entire length of the centre sprig, spilling scores of glasses of wine and scattering flowers and ornaments liberally over the guests! An elephant couldn't have done much more damage!

At the very end of the sprig he paused, exhausted, but was galvanised into action when some well-meaning Distiller took another grab at him, possibly in an attempt to halt the rising cost of demolition. Probably now convinced that the whole world was his enemy, Mickey rocketed into the kitchen, only to crash full-tilt into and overturn, an antique wooden nest of fillets of beef, covered with herbs, which until that moment had been destined for the oven!

Ironically, on Burn's Night, best laid plans had "ganged astray"!

Mickey was last observed speeding through the basement pursued by an apoplectic chopper waving Chef! Against all odds, though, he lived for a couple more years and died peacefully.

His successors have, so far, not copied his sleeping habits but it is always worth checking the punch-bowls before the start of any proceedings at Vintners' Hall.

---

76. That snot the way to treat the fans

In my twenty four year stint as a boxing M.C. I met hundreds of boxers great and small; introducing them to the cheering crowds either as contestants or as pre-main event Celebrities.

Muhamed Ali was wonderful, Mike Tyson positively sinister, Henry Cooper and Frank Bruno so friendly and Barry McQuigan shyly religious.

There were others, however, in this brutal sport who to me are also very memorable. Boxers who didn't quite make it to the top but who nevertheless gave the fans real value.

Notably one Stan McDermott. Stan invariably knocked out his opponent or was himself knocked out; his contests very often saw him staggering around almost out on his feet only to catch his opponent with a most violent blow which put him out cold. Or it might be the other way; as Stan had his man really groggy, he might himself collect one on the jaw and pass out – usually very untidily!

This to my mind is the very ingredient of professional boxing that the fans absolutely love to see. Two big brave men, both with knock-out punches, reeling and recovering, striking and staggering. Which way will it go? It can be so exciting.

Very often Stan would be in "The final bout of the evening" and many fans, interested only in the "Main Event" would start making tracks for home, missing Stan's contribution to the evening.

My wife (who loved Stan) and I in fact used to stop any customers we saw about to leave, with the admonition "Don't miss the last fight folks, it'll be the best fun of the evening.".

Many people later thanked us for this advice.

My particular memory of Stan was the night he fought Neville Meade in an Official Eliminator for the Heavyweight Championship of Great Britain at Wembley Arena.

Stan entered the ring first and, as M.C. I greeted him and his trainer, Terry Lawless, to make the usual last minute checks. "You're Stan McDermott, from East Ham. You weigh 15 stone 11 pounds and you agree this contest is for 10 three minute rounds?" They both nodded and I finished by asking "And howya keeping Stan?"

"Alright" he said "except for this blee'nt sinusitis. It makes my life a misery – especially under these floodlights".

"I can help you with that" I said. "Hold on a minute while I check Neville's details".

I went over to Meade's corner to do this only to be greeted with the complaint, "'Ee can't get 'is 'and inta the glove, mate!"

Sure enough Meade's huge hand was too big for what seemed to be a very large glove.

Something had to be done and I announced through the microphone, "May we have a larger pair of gloves for Neville Meade, please? These are too small".

Laughter and catcalls from the 9000 fans and a flurry of waving from near the dressing rooms assured me that action had been initiated, so I went back to Stan.

"Stan" I said, "about this Sinusitis. You know all that stuff you blow into your hanky?"

"What, snot?" he murmured.

"Yes" I replied, "well that catarrh lines the inside of your nose and above along the forehead and if it gets hard, when you're in a smoky, dry atmosphere – like tonight – it causes pain in the optic nerve which runs through the forehead and then along by the temple towards the top of the ear".

"That's exactly where I get these terrible pains" moaned Stan.

"Yes" agreed Dr. Sullivan, "so I'll tell you what you can do – er – hold on a minute Stan, the new gloves have arrived".

Crossing the ring, watched by 9000 pairs of eyes (and a few hundred cauliflower ears!) I murmured to Neville's seconds, frantically trying to get his leg of lamb sized fist into the new glove, "Let's know when you're ready, lads".

"This set's too blee'nt small too!" they choursed.

Astonished, I announced over the microphone "Can we have some even bigger gloves for Meade please. The biggest you've got!"

More frantic signals from the area of the dressing rooms and I knew I had some more time to dispense my valuable medical advice to Sinusitic Stan.

"Now Stan" I advised, "the first thing to do is to soften that hardened catarrh so that it runs away properly down your nose. Put some hot wet towels over your forehead; breath steam up your nose – anything that will melt the hard catarrh and make it drain away".

"That sounds sense" he muttered.

"Believe me Stan it is" I confirmed, "I've seen it work lots of times".

"Hold on – you ready yet Neville ? – let me know!"

"That's not enough though" I continued to Stan, "you've got to stop it all forming up again. So cut out most of your starchy foods that cause the catarrh, like bread, cheese, spuds, rice, biscuits and those you do eat, chew very thoroughly. Best to eat nothing but fruit for a few days really. And don't have any milky drinks to go to bed on".

"Blimey – I 'ave Orlicks every night" says Stan.

"Worst thing you can do" says the State Registered M.C. over his shoulder as he spies over to the enemy corner "You done yet, lads?"

"Just tying up" came the welcome shout.

"Remember Stan, hot towels, knock off the starchy foods and eat tons of fruit. You'll need about a week".

"Thanks Gov." said my hero.

A signal from Meade's corner, a thumbs up from the Timekeeper, a glance from the Referee entering the ring, a go-ahead wave from the B.B.C. television crew and I launched into my official announcement.

"My Lords, Ladies and Gentlemen. We now come to the final bout of the evening. A contest of ten rounds, three minutes each round, an official Eliminator for the Heavyweight Championship of Great Britain.

Presenting, from – East Ham, Stan McDermott and from Swansea, Neville Meade.

At the weigh-in today McDermott scaled fifteen stone eleven pounds, Meade sixteen stone six pounds.

Your Referee for this contest is Mr. Sid Nathan and your Timekeeper is Mr. Tom Powell".

The bell rang and the two heavy punchers sprang at each other for what proved to be a most exciting contest.

It finished in the 5th round when Meade (who later became the not-very-well-known British Heavyweight Champion) caught Stan a peach of a right hander which hurled him back into the corner padding. There to collapse very ungracefully, like a sixteen stone wobbly-legged, flailing-armed cloth doll, to a sitting position – spark out!

I don't suppose Stan can recall much about that fifth round but I sincerely hope he remembers the wise words about Sinusitis – delivered in the centre of the Wembley Arena's floodlit ring whilst 9000 not normally patient boxing fans waited and waited for the start of what was probably his most important fight.

77. Premiereal palpitations

One evening the manager of a small firm of caterers rang to ask me if I could look after a little party being given at a private home in Chester Square late the following night after the London premiere of a film called "Tiara Tahiti". "You'll only be needed for half-an-hour" he said.

"I've promised to take my wife to a show that evening, Sir" I replied. "Can I get you another Toastmaster?"

"What time does your show finish?" He enquired.

"About 10.15 pm".

"Well, that's alright – we won't need you until 11 o'clock. Bring the Missus with you, leave her in the car for half-an-hour and I'll give you a fee big enough to pay for your night out".

It was, as my wife readily agreed, too good to miss, so next night, after the show, I reported at 10.45 pm to the manager at a most beautiful eight-roomed apartment in Chester Square – the home of a newspaper magnate.

It was at the top of a block and had direct access to the roof garden which the magnate had taken over and, at enormous cost, converted temporarily into a miniature South Seas island. I understand the guests were to sit there, watch the dawn come up over London chimney pots, eat food being prepared in "Cannibal" cauldrons set up amid the palm trees, and listen to the music of an Hawaiian band.

The caterer showed me round, told me of the few things he wanted me to do and gave me a list of the guests – a most impressive collection of film stars, ministers and peers. Then almost as an afterthought, he said, "Oh! And they won't be here until after midnight".

"Midnight!" I choked, "What about my poor wife sitting down there in the car?"

"Oops!" he said, "I'd forgotten about her! Don't worry though, I'll get someone to go downstairs in a while and bring her up until the guests arrive".

He was as good as his word because about half-an-hour later, slightly bemused, my wife appeared. She was immediately given the Grand Tour of the apartment (she loved the solid gold taps in the bathroom) and the roof, guided to a deck chair beneath the palms, revived with a glass of champagne and presented with a dish of goulash – served direct from a cauldron.

Suddenly, to our consternation, the famous guests arrived. There appeared to be hundreds of them and every lady seemed to have a mink coat, which in the absence of a cloakroom, she'd dump on the floor at the side of the lift. Soon there was a pile some three feet high – a mountain of mink!

This sight and the near presence of so many stars (Maureen Swanson and I, for example, were for one ecstatic moment jammed together in a doorway) tended to excite me and I must confess I forgot completely about my wife for half-an-hour until the caterer, squeezing by with two pots of caviar, said from a corner of his mouth "I couldn't get your Missus out – I hope she's alright".

My Missus! I was so used to working alone that I hadn't given her a thought. Where the devil was she?

As I searched through hordes of laughing celebrities packed into every room and hallway, our Host the newspaper magnate, provided me with a clue.

"Toastmaster" he said, "there's a woman on the roof I don't recognise. I want you to find out who she is. We may have to call the police".

I gulped hard and said, "Is she short and plumpish, Sir, with fair hair and a yellowish coat?"

"That's her!" he snapped "Who is she?"

To have told the truth would have put my kindly friend the caterer well into the fertilizer trade, so it had to be a lie.

"I think she said she was from one of the newspapers, Sir".

"Well, I didn't invite anyone from the Press" he retorted, "she must be a gatecrasher, or worse".

"Leave it to me, Sir" murmured the efficient Toastmaster, desperately, slipping away in the direction of the roof.

I soon found the gatecrasher. She was sitting with others in a small circle round one of the cauldrons and looking slightly frightened. John Mills was on her right, James Mason on her left and they were all laughing at something the Home Secretary was saying to Moira Lister.

"Excuse me, Madam, "I said, giving her a warning glance, "you're wanted on the telephone. This way, please".

The gatecrasher followed me through the crowds to the lift, where I all but pushed her in. "Ground floor, Madam" I said, in a voice which was half Toastmaster, half very worried husband.

I then kept out of the way for a while, but the magnate found me, demanding, "what happened to that woman?"

"I challenged her Sir", I lied "and she said she was from the 'City Press'. So I escorted her from the premises".

"I didn't want her thrown out" he snapped. "I wanted her detained. Lady Bloggs, (one of his most important guests) says her £30,000 diamond bracelet is missing. That woman was probably a jewel-thief! Get the caterer to help you catch her – she can't have gone far!"

I shot away to the kitchen and blurted out the whole story to the caterer.

"Don't worry, son" he said soothingly, "the silly old cow has probably left it at home. You just shove off, quick".

It didn't seem very satisfactory, but I had been paid and was now being told by my immediate employer to go. So I went.

I was worried though, and so was the great jewel thief, sitting patiently in the car, when I told her. And we stayed worried for the next twenty-four hours, both suffering nightmarish dreams ("Bank of England man's wife accused of big jewel theft") until the Caterer took us off the hook with a 'phone call. "She left it on her dressing table. I told you, didn't I?"

Next time the Missus stays in the car.

78. A day in dear old Ireland

During a visit to Limerick Town in 1969 my wife and I decided, on impulse, to drive to Ballybunnion, just because we were intrigued by its funny name.

We were out of town very quickly and on to the lovely, empty country roads; so empty in fact that for most of the time we were on our own, becoming slightly annoyed if ever another car appeared in our rear view mirror! The solution would be to stop, let the intruder overtake and then wait until he'd absolutely disappeared up the road ahead before we'd start again.

Once, after stopping in this way, I was so affected by the peace and silence that I asked my wife if she'd stay in the parked car and let me walk a mile ahead before coming to pick me up.

It was marvellous! Pure silence and fresh, scented air! The only sound I heard, when perhaps half a mile up the road, was a moo from a cow in some far distant field. Heaven!

Nearing our destination, with the hedges on either side of the road turning into great fuchsia bushes (miles of them) we came to a 'T' junction where the two road signs, pointing right and left <u>both</u> said, "Ballybunnion".

It was Ireland after all – and my wife remarked that she was beginning to understand what was strange with my family.

Anyway, I chose to go to the right and we soon came to the nice little seaside resort of Ballybunnion, where, after a look around we happened upon the 'World Famous

Ballybunnion Seaweed Baths' in some Nissan huts tucked away at the top of the beach near the small cliffs.

"What are these baths good for?" I enquired of the stout old biddy who was in charge.

"What do you suffer from?" came the cheery response.

Thus persuaded(!) I took a Seaweed Bath – one of the most enjoyable experiences of my life. Lying, on a wrack of seaweed, in a bath of what seemed to be very warm white wine which drew all the tension and toxins from my London-poisoned body, I particularly remember that whenever I raised an arm from the water it was immediately dry.

Ultimately, I floated back to my patient wife, who'd been having a pleasant gossip and tea with the old Irish lady, and managed to coax her into trying the treatment.

When after about an hour she came back to me she looked radiant, calm, serene – and about half a stone lighter. It was the bath she's never forgotten.

On the way back to the hotel, we decided to record the lack of traffic in County Limerick by counting every car which passed on the other side of the road. We did this meticulously, even while stopping to go silly over a little Irish donkey which had a dog and a cat on its back – owner nowhere in sight! But this was Ireland.

The final count, including the evening rush hour traffic leaving Limerick Town was 89 cars! In two hours, in the 47 miles from Ballybunnion, that's all we saw! (I can see more than 89 cars parked in my roadway any weekday!)

There were still more memories to be garnered from that day —- . During a pre-dinner drink at the hotel we asked the barman if he knew where we could obtain a couple of the small, clear, jug-shaped glasses they used for their soft drinks. He said he'd make enquiries and within a few minutes came to our table, whispered "Give us a quid" and gave us six glasses wrapped in a copy of the 'Limerick Recorder'.

Whether this was an example of Irish hospitality or Irish criminality has worried me slightly over the past thirty years but not affected my fondness for the glasses, all six of which we still retain in perfect condition.

We call the glasses 'The Moonies' because that very night we, and millions of other viewers, watched spellbound as the first man stepped on to the moon.

Altogether, as my Irish ancestors might have said, "A broth of a day!"

---

79. If I were rich

It's not only the money, the food, wines and the fascinating people and events that make Toastmastering interesting for me, it's the extra little memories.

One night at the fabulous Inn on the Park Hotel after a party to launch the Malaysian Air Services flights from London, I was asked to stop each lady on her way out with a somewhat officious, "Please wait here, Madam" and then, whilst she was still bristling slightly, tap on a door behind me.

This was the signal for a gorgeous young Malaysian air-hostess to emerge carrying a large bouquet (some forty stems each with perhaps six blooms) which she presented to the now astonished guest, with the words, "Malaysian orchids for a pretty lady".

This was a marvellous way to say good night to lady visitors – their delirious joy on being given some two hundred and forty orchids was really something to see (imagine it

happening to your wife) and we had this very pleasant duty at least two hundred times. Understandably it made us very happy too.

As with all P.R. occasions more people were invited than turned up. After the guests had gone there were still plenty of bouquets left, neatly spread out on the floor of the side room. Just lying there, each worth at least £40.00 in money – more in happiness.

An air-hostess gave one to my wife, who had come to collect me, and the organiser gave me another one, in lieu of a tip. He wondered if we could find homes for the others and I said the cloakroom girls might like some. We therefore trooped <u>into</u> the Ladies' Powder Room, all giggly, made our presentations and left three stout, elderly ladies as starry-eyed as brides.

There were still two dozen or so bouquets left and the organiser asked me if I knew any more ladies who might like orchids. Never without cheek, I said I had a flower-loving mother, two neighbours who had just gone to hospital and an Office full of pretty girls. He promptly gave me another four bouquets.

My mother and the two ladies in the hospital were of course, over the moon with their orchids. The ward more or less erupted with interest and joy. Two hundred and forty orchids, all at once. We surely hastened a few recoveries in that ward.

The girls at the Bank were no less pleased; I gave them each an orchid with a few whispered, lying words and within moments there was a bubble of "orchid" happiness around the normally staid office. I understand it spread to the luncheon club and coffee rooms, too.

The best moments came, however, when with a few orchids left over I started to give them to elderly ladies in the street. A charlady emptying a bucket in a Cannon Street gutter will never (she assured me) forget her brief moment with a bank clerk; nor will a coloured Traffic Warden in Watling Street who made me pin the bloom on her bosom. Nor will I, for these were moments of pure, simple happiness.

The only slight hitch occurred when, in buying my "Evening News" outside the St. Paul's station, I presented my last double orchid to the lady paper-seller. She was overwhelmed, stopped everything and insisted I wait to see what it looked like pinned on. This took only seconds but it was rush-hour and a queue built up from which about twenty places back, a nasty, non-romantic navvy called "Oi, Romeo – get a bleedin move on".

If I were rich I'd do this often; any millionaire who doesn't give away orchids in the street a couple of times a week isn't getting value out of his money.

80. Loading and unloading is two different things

In early 1943, as a very new Sub-Lieutenant in Combined Operations, I was involved in some test firings of the Army's then new Bofors Guns, from landing craft.

We brought our ten craft on to a river beach at low tide to find soldiers lined up on the shore ready with their ten Bofors.

We let down our ramps and the soldiers manhandled one gun on to each landing craft. We then closed the ramps, came astern and were away towards the sea. No bother, and I was very pleased with the efficiency of my ten small teams.

At sea, with the aid of a light plane towing a drogue target, the soldiers practised firing their new wonder guns. Was there too much movement, even in calm seas, in these small, shallow-drafted landing craft? Would the vibration of the firings shake the bottom out of the vessel? Was there an all-round arc of fire against aircraft?

About three uncomfortable hours later, having proved that the guns wouldn't be accurate in choppy seas, that we hadn't had the bottom shaken out of our craft and that only a 270° arc of fire was possible without blowing the coxswain's head off, we turned for home. Hungry, cold, wet sailors; hungry, cold wet and seasick soldiers. All longing to get ashore.

Arriving back in the river we found it difficult to recognise our beach. The full tide had come in (although starting to ebb quite swiftly) and at the spot where we'd beached ten landing craft for the pick-up there was now room for only one. Just one mound of sand, almost like a small hill.

Signalling for the other nine craft to stay in line ahead in the middle of the narrow river, facing inland against the ebbing tide, I instructed my own coxswain to take us in and unload the gun and the soldiers as quickly as he could. I could foresee trouble if the other craft, with their inexperienced coxswains were kept 'waiting' overlong in the middle of a narrow, fast flowing river. The trick was to steer into the tide just sufficiently fast to stop themselves being pushed backwards. Then to come in one at a time, unload, get out and let the next craft do the same.

As we came in I was instructing not only my own coxswain but the other nine and things were getting a little hairy – especially out there in the middle of the river – with landing craft beginning to point in all directions!

My advice to my own coxswain was to come in fast and slide on to the beach with the craft facing slightly towards the sea and to keep his engines running forward at slow speed. (This to save the stern being swept seaward by the tide). I also warned him that, as the heavy Bofors Gun was pulled off, and he felt us rise sharply in the water, he should immediately, by putting his Higgins Remote Control Gear Stick back hard, go astern, while our two seamen were raising the ramp. As I would be occupied keeping an eye on the rest of my flock, I would leave it to him to look astern and steer the craft out, being careful not to crash into the others, now performing some weird gyrations in mid-river.

It worked well and in the midst of my yelling advice to the meandering nine, I felt the craft rise and heard the Higgins Remote Control Gear go hard astern. "Up ramp" I roared to the seamen, without glancing around.

"Can't raise ramp, sir! The Colonel's on it".

I turned forward, astonished. There was the Colonel, an immaculate English gentleman, standing on the ramp, murmuring something like, "I say, Old Boy!"

"Sorry, Colonel" I spluttered, signalling appropriately to the coxswain, "we'll take you back in!"

Simultaneously, two things happened. The coxswain pushed his Higgins Remote Control Gear Stick forward, hard, and the Colonel, with a cry of "Don't bother!" stepped off the ramp into what he probably thought was six inches of water, and went down about ten feet! And, as the top of his tin helmet vanished under water, the ramp passed over him!

"Full astern" screamed your truly, with visions of having to take a corpse home from his first worthwhile exercise.

Back crashed the Higgins Remote Control Gear Stick, shooting the craft astern and "Glory be!" the Colonel popped up.

"My fault, Old Boy" he called and with a wave, and some help from his giggling soldiers, he was away – leaving me to get the other nine craft in.

I think I managed it, but if you are ever up one of those little rivers on the Essex coast and find a Bofors gun, or even a Higgins Remote Control Gear Stick, just leave it – please!

81. The real decision

During preparations for the celebrations of the 50th Anniversary of the of the 'D Day' landings in Normandy, it has suddenly struck me that, in a life in which I've taken many seemingly important decisions several on occasions well in the public eye on television, (like being M.C. at the riot after the Hagler/Minter Middleweight Championship of the World with its 460 million viewers, or Toastmaster at the Lord Mayor's Banquet) the most important was taken in 1944, when I was but twenty-four years old.

I was at that time a Sub-Lieutenant in a flotilla of fifteen Landing Craft, Assault, (LCA's) attached to the Landing Ship, Infantry, 'Empire Crossbow'. Our job, together with hundreds of other LCA's was to ferry troops in for the initial assault on Normandy.

As the first wave on 'Gold' beach, the earliest invaded beach of the British sector, we had been told we could expect 50% fatalities. Usually the Wardroom was given estimates of casualties. Very cheerful!

We were confined to ship, lying in the Solent for several weeks before the big day. Then came the briefing, the loading of the assault troops and, after a tense twenty-four hour delay during which three poor chaps went insane, the crossing to Normandy.

My briefing had been very clear. Our ship would heave to, six miles off the Normandy coast, and the soldiers would be loaded, thirty-three at a time, into our fifteen landing craft which were then to be lowered.

My Lieutenant would take ten of our craft in, carrying "A" and "B" Companies of the 1st Battalion, Royal Hampshire Regiment, leaving me with the other five carrying "C" Company of the 1st Battalion, Dorsetshire Regiment which I had to amalgamate with five carrying "D" Company of the 1st Dorset's from a sister ship, the "Empire Spearhead". We ten craft should then follow, at 1800 Revs., Motor Launch No. 131 fitted with the very latest in radar equipment. This would head absolutely straight to our beach and would be aided by seaward signals from a midget submarine "X 20" secretly "parked" in a positively accurate position one mile off the beach for the past forty-eight hours. The Motor Launch would take us half-a-mile past the submarine and then turn away, leaving us to roar in on exactly the same course, stopping for nothing and hitting the beach at full speed, to ensure we stayed there sufficiently firmly to let all the troops off.

By way of incidental information, we were told that our troops were to take a German strongpoint slightly to the West of a wrecked wooden ship stranded on our particular stretch of beach. There was no guarantee that the wreck would still be there by the time we came in, as some of the bombardment shells and rockets might fall short and blow it to pieces; if it survived, however, it could be a good land mark for the soldiers.

So ... we arrived off the Normandy coast. It was rougher than we'd ever known for landing craft manoeuvring (Gold Beach had the worst weather of all five beaches), but, after a few nightmares during the lowering process (one of my men had two fingers torn off) we formed up and started to follow the Motor Launch. This was it – and the more imaginative among us began to wonder if this was to be our last journey.

My craft carried the senior Major in charge of the three hundred and thirty very highly trained soldiers that we were taking in. We were very glad to have him aboard. He was everyone's idea of a hero; tall, broad, handsome and icy calm – just the sort of chap you need when you're beginning to get a bit excited yourself. He won the Military Cross about an hour later -.

THE NORWEGIAN SHIP "MARCIA"

WRECKED IN A TEMPEST AT LES ROQUETTES, NORMANDY IN JANUARY 1882
USED AS LANDMARK BY 553RD LCA FLOTILLA WHEN TAKING THE 1ST DORSETS INTO THE
INITIAL ASSAULT ON THE NORMANDY BEACHES ON 6TH JUNE 1944

We passed the tiny submarine and sped on, to applause from a lonely figure in its conning tower. Then the Motor Launch turned away. Half a mile to go …

Soon we were near enough to discern the shapes of fortified houses and concrete pillboxes on shore. It was getting very exciting. Rockets were being fired, four hundred a time, over our heads from the Landing Craft, Rockets, just astern of us, and heavy shells were whistling over like express trains.

Planes were zooming in from the East, the North and the West and on our left in line with us, roaring in like a wave of surf, were the landing craft from the other ships in Force G.

At about this point, the soldiers in my boat asked my permission to smoke. What discipline! For all they knew we were all within minutes of death. As Toastmaster I've given 'permission to smoke' at thousands of banquets since then, but never so emotionally as on that day!

"The old wreck should be out there on the left" said the Major, pointing slightly to port. "Can you see it?"

"No, I can't Sir", I replied, "but it might have been blown up!"

"I'd feel more comfortable if I could see some part of it", he grunted.

We continued to scan the beach – he from his six-foot odd, me from about four-foot-two (I had less pluck than he, but perhaps more sense, and was crouching!) and then we both gasped, "It's over there" pointing to the right.

The blasted wreck was well over to starboard! All the pinpointing by the midget submarine, all the state of the art radaring by the Motor Launch and we were a quarter of a mile to the East of where we should have been! It was the weather of course.

I looked at the Major and he looked at me. He knew I had absolutely rigid instructions to go straight in after the Motor Launch peeled off and I now strongly suspected that if we did so, we would land his men some four hundred yards to the left of the strongpoint they were supposed to wipe out.

Strict naval training had reinforced my innate respect for authority and then, as now, I did not lightly disobey orders …

"Can we be sure Sir?" I asked him.

In reply he showed me his picture of the wreck, taken by the RAF a few days earlier. There was no doubt. That was our wreck, well over to starboard instead of slightly to port.

A few moments of absolute torment, with visions of very brave men being needlessly mined, sniped at or even set alight as they ran along the four hundred yards of exposed, mined beach and then I shouted to my signalman, "Signal a ninety degree turn to starboard!"

"We can't do that Sir, we've … !"

"DO IT!!" I roared at the poor nineteen-year old.

He raised a green flag on a short stick and we waited impatiently for the coxswains of the other nine craft to acknowledge that they understood the order by raising their right hands. Eventually, after a lot of shouting and cursing across the water, they did.

"Execute!" I screamed.

Down came the flag and all my ten boats turned to the right, crashing into waves that had been previously, and more comfortably, on our starboard quarter, and heading, it seemed, towards the Atlantic rather than France!

The Major grunted approval and he and I listened sardonically to shouts like, "What's the silly bastard doing now?" or more kindly, "Going home chums?" coming faintly across the wind and water.

I said to him "We'll keep our eye on that wreck Sir, and when we're level, I'll turn. That's if we can get level".

"Thanks" he replied – and I felt calmer and more prepared to explain to the Court of Inquiry which I was now sure I'd have to face.

After what felt like hours but was probably about five minutes, we seemed about level with the wreck. "Say when", I said, "and I'll give the order".

He waited another eternity (perhaps thirty seconds) and then said "Now will do, I think, old boy".

"Ninety degrees to port " I roared to the signalman.

Up went his hand with a red flag; up went the hands of the other nine coxswains.

"Execute!"

Down went the flag and we all turned for France, increasing to 1900 revs to try to arrive on the beach at the same time as the other groups, none of which had altered course. Shells and mortar bombs exploded in the water about ten yards directly ahead of us and again about ten yards astern, but that was all apart from some small arms fire and then we were through, straight to the beach.

The Major and his men, these strangers we'd never seen before and would probably never meet again, dashed (or if seasick we carried) ashore at exactly the place they needed to be, and we headed back to sea to pick up more soldiers.

Just a tiny incident in a day of thousands of major incidents – but it was the greatest <u>real</u> decision of my life.

118

After a period of some forty five years I visited the Normandy Beaches again to find out more about what we'd done that day. I discovered that:

1. We'd landed on the beach at Les Roquettes to the east of the tiny village of Le Hamel.

2. Our wooden-ribbed wreck, which had floundered in 1888 was still there. We learned from an old book that she was the "Martia".

3. Our soldiers, the 1st Hampshire's and the 1st Dorset's, were on their third initial assault on an enemy beach within 11 months.

4. They were the furthest to the right on Gold Beach which in turn was the furthest right of the British beaches; thus they were in the Army's Position of Honour.

5. They were the first British Infantry ashore that day.

6. One of their D. Day objectives was the small fishing port of Arromanches. The Hampshire's captured it by 9.00 p.m. and, within a few hours, the first units of Port Winston, the great artificial harbour, were towed in for assembly there. Its early capture had thus been absolutely vital.

7. My very gallant Major was Major Robert Nicoll who survived the war and is still alive, in Devon where I hope to visit him later this year.

8. Every one of the many books and articles I've read about the landings, stresses that all the shallow drafted Landing Craft on each of the five beaches were pushed by wind and tide to the East of the planned landing places.

9. My ten L.C.A's, thanks to that dear old wreck, were possibly the only ones which landed exactly where they were supposed to.

82. What did you do in the war, Daddy ?

In April 1939 Italian troops invaded Albania and very quickly overwhelmed this tiny Balkan state.

The Italians then, in a 1930's version of ethnic cleansing, moved large numbers of Albanian families from strategic towns and replaced them with families shipped across the Adriatic from Italy.

The second World War started later that year with Albania under the control of the Italians and later the Germans and it was not until mid-1945 that the Allies liberated the poor backward country.

In common with the most awkward and unreasonable Yugo-Slavs, the Albanians didn't seem terribly grateful to their liberators. Their main reaction was to demand that we, the British Army and Navy, immediately remove from their sacred land all Italian troops and civilian families.

We, the silly old British, agreed to this, of course, and that is how I came to find myself in the harbour of Durrazo, standing on the bow of H.M. Landing Ship Tank 77 looking shoreward at the amazing sight of about 25,000 very scruffy Italians, led by the red-scarfed Garibaldi troops, edging in single file towards the ship.

Their progress was so slow that I went ashore to see what was holding them up. I found it to be another form of cleansing! A British Army sergeant, armed with a stirrup pump spray, was squatting on a three legged stool beside a large bucket of D.D.T. powder and, as the Italians filed by, dropping their trousers and raising their upper garments so as to expose their armpits, giving each of them three strong puffs of D.D.T., one under each arm and one in the nether region.

After watching this fascinating procedure for some minutes, I blurted to the sergeant "We don't half get some funny jobs, sarg. What the hell are a couple of ordinary London boys doing in Albania, fumigating Italians and taking them back to Italy?"

He looked up at me with a weary smile (he'd fumigated about 500 and had over 24,000 to go) and said "Yus! This ain't the job I signed on for, Sir!" Then added, "But it's got its moments; jus nah I gave the usual two puffs, an when I looked dahn for the third it was different! But I gave it to _her_ just the same!"

We eventually loaded two thousand of the dejected, smelly-but-well-fumigated bodies on to our ship.

While we were still tied to the shore, closely scrutinized by the scowling, threatening Albanians, who hated their former conquerors, our passengers were very quiet indeed. Hushed in fact.

The moment we cast off, however, and were no more than two feet from the quay, a great Italian cheer rent the air, Italian flags were plucked from tunics and blouses and raised high whilst the Italians marched up and down singing patriotic songs.

The marching and singing lasted until we passed the harbour mouth into the open sea – which was very rough. It used to be said that our shallow-drafted L.S.T's would roll on wet grass and the poor wretches immediately became very sick indeed.

None were more sick than the 25 very pregnant women amongst our passengers and to me (as Welfare Officer deputising for the Sick Berth Attendant who was "D.C.A." or Disease- Caught-Ashore – a euphemism for V.D.) fell the task of tying these poor ladies, still itching from the D.D.T. powder, still vomiting heavily, into stretchers and then, with the aid of their excitable, screaming, vomiting husbands, tying the stretchers to any rigid part of the heavily rolling ship.

During the 24 hour voyage to Taranto (the Anus of Italy) we had trouble in the open bridge when unexplained small "rocks" appeared on our navigational charts. These proved to be fleas, sucked from the 1000 people huddled in the tank space (a 208 foot long garage which formed our lower deck) as soon as our giant fume clearing fans were turned on, and thrown up into the air.

Previous experience of carrying primitive refugees had forced us, on medical grounds, to deny the passengers access to the crew's "heads" (toilets) and the ship's carpenter was ordered by the Captain to construct a scaffolded arrangement hanging out from the port bow for the passengers' requirements. We high up in the bridge could see them sitting over the side, holding on like grim death as the ship tossed and rolled and regularly being drenched by the bow wave. They were going back home but it wasn't very nice.

As we neared Taranto it became apparent that coming alongside the quay there, as ordered, and disembarking our passengers over the side via rope ladders, would be fraught with problems. The Captain therefore dispatched a rather unusual naval signal to the Port Authorities (a copy of which I still have) which said, "Owing to considerable number of pregnant women amongst passengers suggest berth at L.S.T. Hard on arrival". (The Hard being a specially constructed part of the harbour where L.S.T's could come in head first, as on to a beach, open their bow doors and lower the bow ramp so that passengers could walk off).

Almost inevitably the signal was garbled in transmission and "berth" became "birth!"

Twenty four hours later we were back in Durrazo. There were still long lines of Italians and my friend the cockney sergeant was still giving them the old "one, two three!"

120

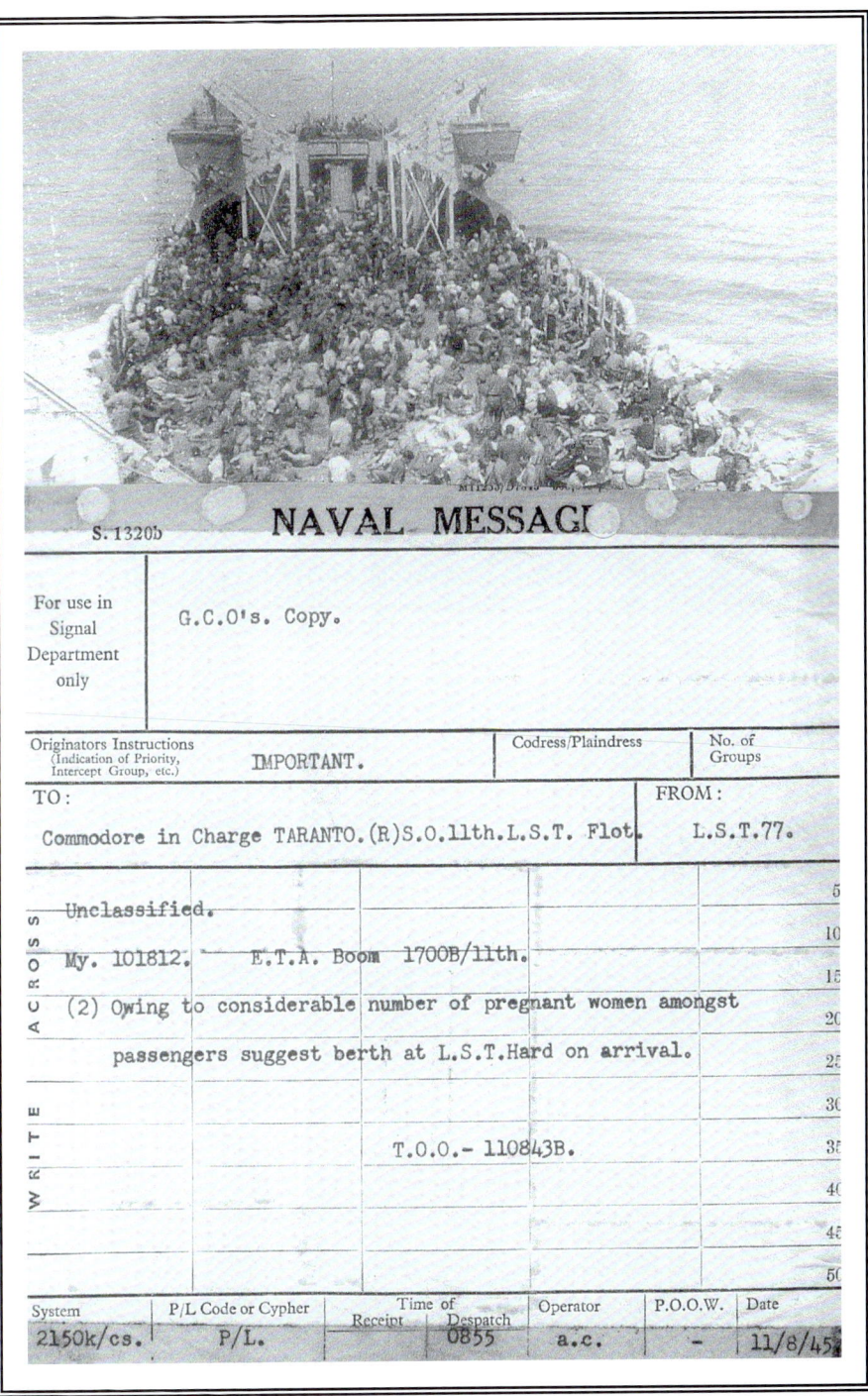

S.1320b

NAVAL MESSAGE

For use in Signal Department only	G.C.O's. Copy.

Originators Instructions (Indication of Priority, Intercept Group, etc.)	IMPORTANT.	Codress/Plaindress	No. of Groups

TO:	FROM:
Commodore in Charge TARANTO.(R)S.O.11th.L.S.T. Flot.	L.S.T.77.

Unclassified.

My. 101812.   E.T.A. Boom 1700B/11th.

(2) Owing to considerable number of pregnant women amongst

passengers suggest berth at L.S.T.Hard on arrival.

T.O.O.- 110843B.

System	P/L Code or Cypher	Time of Receipt	Despatch	Operator	P.O.O.W.	Date
2150k/cs.	P/L.		0855	a.c.	-	11/8/45

121

83. All good things come to an end

My final appointment in the Navy was as First Lieutenant of the great naval base at Gibraltar. The War had finished but, because of the great sea traffic through there of ships and sailors on demobilisation, the base was probably as busy as it had ever been. Moreover, I seemed to be very short of staff to help me with my eighteen hours per day tasks.

Suddenly, however, it was Pay Day and I was faced by a workforce of some eight hundred jolly Jack Tars who'd come from the various far flung posts like Signal and Radar Stations and gun sites all round the Rock.

Puzzled, I asked the Fleet Master-at-Arms for a copy of the Pay List. He produced this in fairly quick time but I sensed he was not too pleased to have to pass over such sensitive information.

Basically trying to find perhaps ten extra seamen to help my hard-worked Buffer (Chief Petty Officer) and the three A/B's who slaved with him to keep the ancient base ship, "H.M.S. Cormorant," clean and bright, I was astounded to see the great number of exotic-sounding jobs being done on the Rock and called upon the Master at Arms to explain them to me.

"Master," I enquired mischievously, "what for instance does the Master at Arms Personal Servant do?"

He was instantly defensive "You know Sir, that each Fleet Master-at-Arms is entitled, under King's Regulations and Admiralty Instructions, to have a Personal Servant – who can also help in the office?"

I didn't of course, but had to be careful with this very senior, regular Navy man who knew a lot more about the Regulations and the workings of Gibraltar Base than I did.

"O.K. Master" I cooed, "keep your servant. But what about this 'Prisoner's Friend?' What does he do?"

"Well, Sir" answered the Master, now looking considerably less tense, "he's the man who acts like a warder to the prisoners. Ever since that prisoner cut his wrists last year, the Friend has to make sure that the cutlery is taken away immediately the prisoner has eaten his meals."

(I felt some affinity with this mysterious 'Friend'. I was, after all, the chap who actually sentenced the prisoners to up to seven days in the very ancient, close-barred cells on our old wooden ship).

"Well, Master, I'll interview him for a start" I said crisply. "Send him in to me tomorrow morning."

The 'Prisoner's Friend' turned out to be a good-looking, fresh faced young seaman of the type used in Admiralty recruiting posters.

"Sit down Jack" I said, "I'm calling in lads like you to find out exactly what sort of job you have to do. (He looked a little apprehensive). You know the Navy is trying to get the boys home for demobilisation and I'm trying to help. Now, could I ask you to describe your day's work as the 'Prisoner's Friend?"

"Well, Sir" he said "at 08.30 I take down the prisoner's breakfast."

"Yes?"

"Then, at 09.00, I collect the prisoner's dirty plate and knife and fork; you know Sir, because of that suicide attempt we mustn't leave him with a cutting blade".

"Yes – I heard about that" I said – but I was also thinking about the Buffer's three overworked matelots who, by 09.00 had already put in three solid hours of work.

"And what next?" I coaxed him.

"Well, Sir, at 12.00 I take down the prisoner's lunch."

"Yes?"

"And at 12.30, Sir, I collect the plate and knife and fork."

"In case he attempts to damage himself of course … and what next, his tea and cake?"

"Yes, Sir, – that's at 16.00 and I clear at 16.30."

"Then, I suppose, at about 18.30 you take down his dinner and at 19.00 you clear it?"

"Yes, Sir."

We were both smiling a bit now and I said, quite gently, "Not a bad old job eh Jack?"

"Yes, very nice Sir" he admitted.

"And how many prisoners have we in the cells at the moment?"

"Well —- actually —- none Sir."

He looked at me and I looked at him; (I'll always remember those wise looks we gave each other) and then we both broke into great peals of laughter!

Recovering slightly, I returned to duty.

"Well, Jack, you know that all good things must come to an end?" He nodded pleasantly and understandingly. "Well, tomorrow, report to the Buffer at 06.00 for scrubbing duties …".

Oh that all redundancy-type interviews could be settled as amicably as that one!

I carried on the interviews until my own demobilisation some four months later, questioning men like 'Pants', the pantry man and his assistant, 'Underpants' and succeeded, with help from the Navy's own demobilisation programme, in cutting out some three hundred jobs.

I've been worried about staffing in the Nationalised Industries ever since.

---

84. Quiet night out with Rosie

17th July 1986

It's Big Fight Night at Wembley. Nine bouts. My colleague is M.C. for six of them and I'm doing the three Main Events.

The Main Event itself is being televised to North and South America and Europe with an estimated viewing public of 176 million people and I am getting excited at the prospect.

During the six "undercard" bouts there was possibly as much excitement outside the ring as there was inside. Gangs of tanked-up young men were suddenly rushing down noisily from the cheaper seats, in numbers too many for the police and stewards to apprehend, and taking over the empty ringside seats (£125 each) whose wealthy owners were, as usual, staying in the bar until nearer the Big Fight.

Then, possibly feeling the effects of the tanking-up and not wishing to run the gauntlet of police to get to the toilets and back, very many of the yobs were seen to be standing on the chairs, proudly urinating. It was that sort of night.

My instructions, from Home Box Office, the Great US T.V. Company who were everybody's paymasters that night, were to watch their "Top Gun" man very intently once the Champion and the Challenger were in the ring and gloved up. He would raise his hand at the very moment he heard the T.V. satellite come on station, keep it up whilst the 40 second $500,000 commercial was beamed to the Americas and Europe and then flash it down as a signal that I should make my announcement to those 176 million fight fans.

After a few admonitions that I must watch the great man's raised hand extremely closely and start my announcement immediately he slammed it down (every second costs thousands of dollars), I managed to convince him that I fully understood and would comply.

The great moments began to evolve. First Frank Bruno, the World Heavyweight Champion was escorted down the very long path from the dressing rooms to the ring and as he neared it I raised a tremendous cheer for him merely by announcing his arrival.

Then we looked back toward the dressing rooms for a sight of the Challenger Tim Witherspoon, and waited … and waited … and waited. It's an old trick to keep your tensed up opponent waiting … but twelve minutes of waiting was excessive, wicked, unfair and made the crowd very angry; and it was certainly having the desired effect on Bruno's nerves!

Suddenly there was a burst of noise from the dressing room end of the stadium and the searchlight beams swung there to reveal a group of great big black men each, somewhat incongruously, waving a tiny stars and stripes flag. Round these giants was a ring of London policemen whose shiny helmet tops were flashing in the searchlights. And somewhere in the centre of them all was the Challenger Tim Witherspoon.

From my position in the elevated ring erected in the centre of the sacred Wembley football pitch, I had a wonderful view and, in truth, thought it was all very much over the top. Who at a British venue would need such protection?

I couldn't have been more wrong! Without warning chairs were being thrown at the floodlit group! Some of these, of the light folding metal type, went over them as they progressed towards the ring, hitting guests on the other side of the gangway who then bad-temperedly threw them back; others were deflected by the police and some hit the black minders, but thanks to their strong arms no chair reached Tim Witherspoon the intended victim.

After what seemed a violent eternity, Witherspoon got to the ring. I announced his entry. "Please give a warm Wembley welcome to the Challenger" and was pleasantly surprised at the hearty cheer this produced. A moment or two before it had seemed half of them were trying to cripple or even kill him.

Whilst the boxers were traditionally being gloved-up in the ring, it was my very proud duty to introduce the Celebrities; a great host of current and former World, Commonwealth, European and British Champions. During this Jarvis Astaire, (Vice Chairman of Wembley and an associate of promoters Mickey Duff and Mike Barrett) was constantly (as was his wont) urging me to introduce Mohamed Ali. So much so that I had to break off to tell him that I had a plan for that introduction and would he please trust me!

Ultimately, as the last introduction, I produced, "Those two great adversaries and now great friends, Mohamed Ali and Henry Cooper!" Which produced the loudest and most prolonged applause of the evening.

It was now time to get on with the real business of the evening, the Big Fight. The atmosphere in the Stadium was electric and, I imagine, it was the same in millions of homes across the Western World. I therefore looked in the direction of Top Gun who was to give me the warning and then the signal to start.

Panic! I couldn't see him at his station down by the ring near Witherspoon's corner. The eight black giants were prancing about, waving their tiny flags and obliterating my view! I was reduced to bending and trying to look through their oak-tree legs, still with no success, when Mike Barrett, sensing my trouble, climbed up on to the ring apron and called "What's up M.C.?"

"I can't see Top Gun. He is supposed to signal me" I hissed.

"Don't worry" said Mike, "I can see him and I'll pass on the signal".

So, very tense, I waited. Forty-three thousand boxing fans in the Stadium waited too … but one of them was calling urgently "Bernard, Bernard, BERNARD". It was Jarvis again and I ignored him; I had enough on my plate and wanted no distraction at that particular moment!

"Bernard" chorused other voices, this time from within the ring (it was Bruno's Manager and seconds) "Jarvis is calling you".

I turned and moaned "What? What do you want now?"

"When, you say 'At the weigh-in today' add, 'At the Odeon, Leicester Square' ", he shouted, telling me something I'd already been told by Mike Barrett, Mickey Duff, the Boxing Board of Control Inspector and a special messenger from Jarvis's office. Just the sort of diversion you want as you're about to make an announcement to millions of people!

Before I could scream back "I <u>know</u>," however, Mike Barrett's voice roared, "Bernard!" and I spun towards him. "Go!" he cried.

"What about the warning and the signal" I pleaded, "Top Gun was adamant about that…"

"Do it" screamed Mike "I'm the Promoter. I'm paying you!"

So – I did it. "My Lords, Ladies and Gentlemen, this is a contest for the Heavy weight …"

"Aw No" screamed an American voice from ringside "NOT YET!" Stop, you silly bastard, STOP!"

The silly bastard stopped.

(I understand from my family that Harry Carpenter the B.B.C. Commentator explained that "The Master of Ceremonies has dropped his papers").

A moment or two later, Mike Barrett having vanished and the black guards having been cleared from the ring, Top Gun came in sight, gave me the warning and then the signal and I made my great proclamation to the waiting world. A marvellous experience!

The contest at last got underway. It wasn't one of the most thrilling I'd seen and finished in Round 9 when Bruno sustained a broken jaw – causing the aforementioned yobs to leave their illegally held £125 seats, storm round the barriers which protected the ring and viciously to hurl coins at us.

A pound coin struck my head with some force. I heard a hollow sound (!!) and then felt a warm trickle down my left cheek. I was bleeding!

A shout went up from the wild-eyed drunken yobs, "The M.C.'s been 'urt" and this caused my wife Rosie to confront them, screaming, "Leave him alone – he is a heart patient!"

This brave effort elicited from one member of the mob, the most sensible remark of the evening, "Well if 'ees a blee't 'eart payshun, wot the ell's he doin up there?"

Witherspoon's doctor, who'd jumped into the ring, took one look at my head and said, "You'll have to get that stitched up. Come with me and Frank to Tim's changing room and I'll fix it".

So we started, doctor and two sorry looking patients, down from the ring passing through the excited mob of whom I demanded loudly "Let Frank through, he's hurt bad and he's got to see the doctors, quick" and hoping they would extend the same courtesy to me.

It worked! And soon we were through.

Walking with Bruno across the holy plastic covered Wembley turf, with me trying to comfort him (what can you say to a chap whose broken jaw is hanging down near his shoulders and who has just lost the fabulous title of "Heavyweight Champion of the World?") we were waylaid by two uniformed attendants who told me they had instructions to take Bruno to Witherspoon's changing room and me to "the hospital".

"Hospital?" I said, "I don't want to go to hospital. My wife won't know where I am, how will I get back, will my car be locked in here?"

"It's alright mate", one attendant replied soothingly, "we've got our own 'orspital 'ere in the Stadium and I'll bring yer Missus up to yer".

What a nice surprise! I for one wasn't aware that every great venue is, by law, compelled to have its own hospital.

It turned out to be a small eight-bedded ward with a couple of doctors and nurses who gave their dinner-jacketed, bloody faced new patient an interested welcome.

"You're a bit posh aren't you" said one nurse eyeing my dinner jacket and bow-tie "one of those Lords in the announcements?"

"No, I'm the bloke who made the announcements – your M.C" I said, "and I'm very surprised to find this hospital here. Have you been busy tonight?"

"One heart attack and one broken collar bone" chimed a doctor. "Now up on the table please and let's have a look at your head".

In a couple of minutes during which Rosie was escorted into the ward by the attendant, I was stitched, had a rather large pad fixed on the top of my wound and bandaged right round my head. The doctor then advised a twenty minutes lie down and a cup of sweet tea to which I readily agreed. I'd had a bit of an evening!

During the rest the police 'phoned to inform me that they had caught the coin thrower. Should they charge him or give him a caution? I said "Charge him" so viciously that it hurt my stitches.

Having thanked the very kind medical staff, Rosie and I braced ourselves for the long car journey from Wembley (north west London) to Bromley (south east). It was then about 2 am.

The first problem, we thought, would be to find the car, but this proved easy – it was the only one left in Wembley's vast car park.

Generally relieved we got in, sighed a bit, and I started the engine. "Take it steady, Ben" warned Rosie, "You're very tired and you've been hurt – wait a while".

So we did and out of blue there came a tap on the window. Spinning round we saw a rather simple looking chap who pleaded for a lift towards central London.

"Where do you live?" I queried.

"Catford" he said.

"Blimey" we chorused "you're lucky – we go through there! Get in".

He was lucky, he'd stayed behind a little to try to get some autographs, got lost in the vast stadium, come out to find everything deserted, searched around for buses without success and then by providential guidance re-entered the car park precisely at the time we were getting into our car. He just couldn't believe his luck that we then waited a while.

And, thanks to the bandage he'd thought I was an Indian!

When we explained and he realised that I was the M.C., he got very excited, clamoured for my autograph and told us he'd tell all his work mates how he'd come back from Wembley in the M.C's car.

I felt like some Pop Star, so much so that I stopped in town and bought him a hamburger and then took him right to his front door.

Just another quiet night out with Rosie!

---

85. New York, New York – what a wonderful day!

The private secretary to the Chairman of the Peninsular Company and Oriental Steam Navigation Company rang me recently to enquire whether I would be available to fly to New York and, as she put it, help Sophia Loren during the Banquet and Naming Ceremony for the magnificent new £200m liner, "Crown Princess".

I hesitated. Would my six by-passed old heart be able to take the strain of working so closely with such a voluptuous vision? Would her passionate Italian heart melt publicly at the sight of her red-coated, Bank of England pensioned admirer?

In view of the good money involved we both decided to risk it!!

Arriving at JFK Airport, I was greeted and cosseted by a beautiful uniformed ship's hostess who took me to a stretched limousine, complete with an expatriate English chauffeur, for the journey to Manhattan Docks, on the Hudson River. A decided improvement upon previous visits to New York when transport had been my responsibility.

Logged into a double cabin on the liner replete with every possible luxury, I read a few pamphlets about the ship and learned that although British-owned, she had been built (based on the shape of a dolphin) and was registered, in Italy. She was also Captained, officered and crewed by Italians – with small exceptions like the commis waiters (Philippinos) the sound engineers (Mexicans) and the Reception and Entertainment personnel (British).

On my first night on board, the ship and its wonderful services were given over to Prince Rainier of Monaco, his whole family and a few guests (about 1200!) who were to banquet in aid of the Princess Grace Trust.

This was some gift! Imagine the effort by the crew of receiving so many important people, courteously settling them into their cabins and providing them with a champagne banquet, a champagne cabaret, champagne breakfast and champagne walkabout farewell next morning. They should have had a ginger-beer Toastmaster too, but at the last moment the Chairman decided to keep this luxury for his banquet the following evening.

Next morning we disembarked Prince Rainier's 1200 guests and took on board the 700 guests who were to be supremely spoiled at the Inaugural Banquet and then thrilled at the Naming Ceremony.

Again it was champagne with everything, then a glittering reception, during which Sophia cuddled me warmly (Golly!) after one of my "So Ingleese" announcements, followed by a wonderful Banquet with ye olde English Toastmaster and a fine stalwart Highland Piper.

After the Banquet we invited everyone onto the Promenade Deck as the ship left the Manhattan Docks to the music of a military band and then glided silently along the Hudson River, past the spectacularly illuminated skyscrapers (whose history was brilliantly explained to us, over the Tannoy, by the Cruise Director) on through the dark, warm evening towards the Statue of Liberty, glowing green in the night.

When we reached this lovely, welcoming lady, the ship's siren was sounded as if to salute her; it was, however, a signal to staff on two great barges to commence a fantastic fire-work display just for us.

It was marvellous for guests relaxing there in the warm darkness, sipping champagne as the ship glided along with the Statue of Liberty and the fire-work display on the Starboard side and the superbly illuminated Manhattan skyscrapers on the Port side – but more was to come...

As we turned for home I had to ask the guests to adjourn to the International Show Lounge, situated forward on the 6th and 7th Decks; this was actually in the bow of the ship, where the 6th Deck formed the "Stalls" and the 7th the "Balcony", of a remarkable Theatre. Well I thought it remarkable. Every second seat in the stalls, for instance, had its own tiny table on which, thoughtfully, had been placed a bottle of champagne and two glasses!

This was enough to last the guests through the Cabaret of Tony Bennett and Marvin Hamlisch (no expense spared) and then the lucky devils were free to wander round the fourteen decks of the huge floating palace, taking their pick of casinos, lounges, discos, dance salons, restaurants and pizza bars, all free, all staffed with attentive, courteous staff offering champagne and the most luscious small pizzas I've ever tasted. I went to be bed at about 1.00 a.m. 'pizza-puffed' and left them to it.

The next morning we awoke to find that the ship had moved from Manhattan Docks on the Hudson River to Brooklyn Docks on the East River, i.e. from one side of the famous skyscrapers to the other, ready for the Naming Ceremony.

I went ashore early to seek out the best vantage points, take a general look around and, if possible, get some photographs.

On leaving the ship I had to walk around the stern to the other side of the dock, past what I shall for the moment refer to as a "mystery edifice" and up the other side where, level with the bow of the ship, was a huge scaffolding and plank arrangement of seats (known as a 'Bleacher') for say, a thousand guests.

Accepting from a dockyard matey an expensive, custom built "Princess" souvenir cushion, I found the seat with the very best view, plonked the cushion on it, relaxed and took stock.

In front of me, blocking the mouth of the huge dock were two massive barges. One was empty and flat but completely carpeted in blue, the other was filled with chairs, set cinema style, for the V.I.P's with a small white fenced dais for the Chairman and his party. From the dais a bright blue rope extended to the ship's bow, seemingly miles above and a gang of technicians there were testing both it, and the bottle-releasing mechanism, thoroughly. (Imagine if the bottle failed to break!).

Down below, some Lascar seamen in a rubber float were dabbing white paint on any tiny blobs which had dared show their faces on the Princess.

Behind all this, framing the ship's bow and the barges, in glorious sunshine was the fantastic skyline of Manhattan. The sky was absolutely blue, the East River a lovely green, the New York helicopters were a-buzzing between the skyscrapers and the Staten Island ferries were chugging to and from the Battery. Breathtaking!

The guests from the ship started to arrive at the Bleacher and, having each been given one of the lovely souvenir cushions, were directed to their seats. From my vantage point I watched everything and was able to observe that as the dock workers handed out the cushions, they were throwing some to the rear where accomplices were slipping away with them, into the warehouse behind. (Reminded me of the London Docks!).

Suddenly, in a whisper of excitement, fifteen great stretched limousines arrived with the V.I.P's, people like Carlo Ponti Sophia's husband, the Mayor of New York and the Chairman of the New York Docks and Harbours Board who, amid cheers, were escorted to the seats reserved for them on the barge.

As they were settling in, we heard the distant sound of martial music and, looking to the end of the dock were thrilled to see the full band, and pipers, of Her Majesty's Scots Guards marching to join us.

The effect on the guests (99% American) was terrific. They stood and cheered their heads off – with many bursting into tears. It really was a moving spectacle and, combined with the sight of the beautiful ship, the skyscrapers, the gorgeous blue sky and the passing ships and ferries, tugged at one's emotions.

As the Scots Guards formed up on the second, blue carpeted barge, in a riot of colour, we heard delighted screams from the Italian crew lining the various decks of the ship. They, from their high vantage points, could see that our Guest of Honour was arriving with Sir Jeffrey Sterling (now Lord Sterling) Chairman of P & O, in a horse drawn carriage.

As Sophia drew near and we began to hear the magical clip-clop of the horse's hooves, the crew burst into a lovely Italian song, the sound of which caused her to jump to her feet and join them, waving delightedly. What a day this was turning out to be!

When Sophia had at last, assisted by some tough-looking, but adoring, New York Cops, writhed her way through the V.I.P's and settled her glorious parts into a chair on the dais, we had a few short – and very good – speeches before she was called upon to name the ship.

As her seductive voice purred round the dock, "I name a these sheep 'Crown a Princess a' and God Bless all who a sail in her" she pulled the long blue rope and three things happened. The magnum of champagne crashed on to the bow, the ship's siren blared fit to shake the tops from the skyscrapers and from the now unveiled "Mystery Edifice", came the peals of a full set of church bells especially shipped over from London with a bell ringing team.

A day none of us will forget, I'm sure! How lucky we were to share those magic moments. Some of us were well paid for it too!

And one chap was even cuddled by Sophia Loren!

86. Don't mesh with me

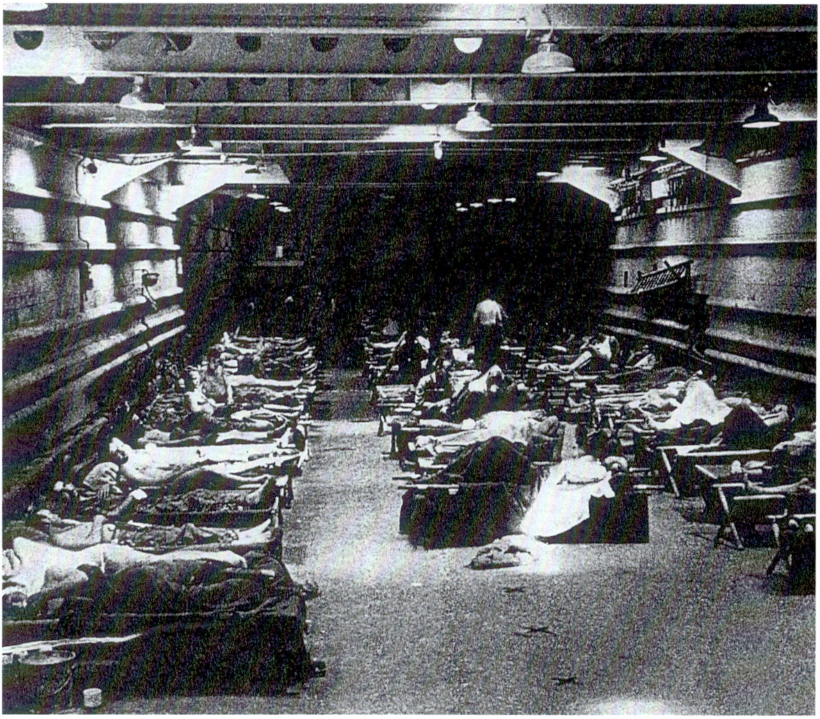

When a Landing Ship Tank comes into a shore it opens its doors and then lowers its great ramp to allow its cargo of heavy tanks and military lorries to disembark on to a beach or perhaps a concrete landing stage.

Often, however, for a variety of reasons, the end of the ramp cannot lie properly and vehicles being driven ashore have to face an eighteen inch drop as they leave the ramp.

Recognising the dangers of this on my L.S.T. we carried a great steel-mesh carpet which we would unroll from half-way along the ramp so that it draped over the end and out well on to the shore, forming a bridge over any 'drop'.

Rolling out this huge monster required the combined strength of about twenty of our crew – who were also needed when the time came to wrap it up again and make it secure before we sailed.

For securing, the rolled-up carpet had to be manhandled to the bulkhead where great wedges were placed under it to stop it moving in heavy seas. Then, to prevent it unrolling, it was also fixed to the bulkhead by a ten foot length of one inch thick wire which had a heavy shackle at its end.

This chain and shackle was a permanent fixture at the end of the carpet, originally intended, I think, for use should the great steel beast ever need to be towed ashore.

All this meant that, whenever the carpet was unrolled down the ramp with its end finally flipping over, the chain and heavy shackle would arc over at about 80 mph with the shackle crashing down on the beach or landing stage.

I'd been in charge of the carpet laying operation on very many occasions and, through experience, knew pretty well where best to stand, just off the ramp, to be near enough to control the efforts of my panting, straining and cursing men but, at the same time far enough away to avoid the speeding shackle.

One day, in the port of Ancona on the east coast of Italy, I watched confidently as the shackle came rushing up and over towards me, knowing it would fall at least a foot short of me.

I heard loud screams of warning from every one of the sailors as the shackle crashed down and wondered why they were (as I thought) panicking. Taking charge in a seaman-like manner, I barked out the usual orders for the completion of the operation.

The job finished, I told the boys to stand down – but many gathered round me with remarks like "That was the coolest thing I've ever seen, Sir" and "Blimey! You must have nerves of steel!" etc.

I modestly thanked them, feeling a little guilty (because I'd <u>known</u> the shackle would fall short of me) but, at the same time reasoning that it wasn't a bad thing for a crew to think their officer was fearless and icy cool in dangerous situations.

I then retired to my cabin for a rest and, before laying down, removed my cap – only to observe that a half-inch square had been gouged from the peak.

Horrified, I fell asleep.

Or did I faint?

87. Hans across the sea

I finished up my wartime career ashore at Gibraltar, in about the best job of my life, as First Lieutenant of the great naval base.

About half way through my five months service there, the Colony was suddenly alive with talk of a young Swiss adventurer who had sailed into the harbour alone in a tiny storm battered boat. His name was Hans Von Mees Teufal, the son of a director of the Swiss Bank Corporation, Gresham Street, City of London, and his call at Gibraltar was his last stop before embarking on a single-handed crossing to New York.

Such a voyage, if achieved in those days, had to be a stupendous feat of navigation, bravery and endurance and I must say we were all thrilled at the prospect of meeting such a hero.

The holder of my privileged post was part of "The Establishment" of the tiny Colony and I was always being invited to some civic or social function or other along with dignitaries like the Chief Justice, the Mayor, the Chief Constable, Chief Librarian, the Coroner etc. Inevitably, because he was invited everywhere during his three week stay, I met Hans many times and must say that my admiration for him began to border on hero-worship. I was not alone in this; the fellow was very big, tough as teak, spell bindingly interesting, amusing, handsome and modest. And he was going to cross the Atlantic alone in a cockleshell of a boat. Most of us, after six years of war, knew that wicked and cruel sea and what she would do to ships and sailors.

The Navy, Army and Air Force on the Rock began to vie with each other to ensure that Hans' crossing would be successful. Our Navy contribution was to get the Base Sailmaker to replace, free, his battered old sails and to fill his larder (and any other space we could find) with lots of dehydrated foods which although not terribly tasty took only about a quarter of the space needed for fresh or canned food.

On the day of his departure great crowds came to wave goodbye to the magnificent but lonely figure in the tiny boat. And as we waved we were filled with emotion and admiration for our daredevil friend.

Two days later, with Hans well into the Atlantic, there came a signal from the Foreign Office, London saying that no Von Mees Teufal had ever been employed at Swiss Bank Corporation, Gresham Street and we should treat our man with suspicion – the probability being that he was an escaping German Prisoner of War!

Months later, after my demobilisation and a six week second honeymoon (which I suppose could equate with Hans' crossing for thrills and exhaustion) I found myself in one of the Bank's ante rooms waiting for my joining interview. Spotting a "Tatler" or "London News", I opened it and there all over the centre-spread was old Hans being feted on his arrival in New York!

Good luck to him! I'm sure he wasn't one of the wicked ones.

88. The long sleep or a brown study

There was one Government Minister, later ennobled, who nearly always looked to be drunk when appearing on television and was usually described as being "indisposed" or "off colour".

He certainly seemed this way many times when I had to look after him at banquets and frankly, I used to feel disgusted that such a boozer was an important part of the team running my country.

He gave me some good memories however, none of which I've put to paper until today and now only because (a) he and his long suffering (and eventually deserted) wife are dead and (b) a 'minder' from the Special Branch Squad has recently informed me that his Lordship wasn't a heavy drinker. It was apparently, that he took pills for his high blood pressure, after which even one drink would set him off…

Perhaps he'd taken the pills and that one drink while preparing to visit the Royal Lancaster Hotel one evening as Principal Guest of a Chartered Institute. Anyway something delayed him sufficiently to make him miss the pre-dinner reception.

When this type of thing happens, a decision has to be made whether we wait for another five or ten minutes (thus upsetting the Chef) or go ahead and announce dinner in the hope that the missing Guest will turn up in the ten minutes it takes us to get the nine hundred guests to their seats!

The President, a smallish, worried man, who clearly sensed that his long cherished Night, and perhaps his World, was collapsing around him, was quite unable to make a decision so the organising secretary, the head waiter and myself (three professionals who'd had experience of his Lordship) made it for him. We'd go ahead – and hope!

Sure enough, eight minutes later, just as I'd got the rank and file to their tables and was forming the President and the V.I.P's into a Procession, his Lordship turned up.

Sprinting down to divest him of his overcoat and hurling it to the cloakroom girl, I breathed "Ah! Good evening, my Lord, just in time. We're forming the Procession and you're leading in with the President".

"Mr President, may I introduce the Right Honourable Lord…"

"Good evening my Lord" beamed the born-again President. "I'm very …"

"I wanna widdle" says our baron.

The toilets were some twenty yards distant and downstairs. Still keen to get Dinner started on time (we had about a minute to spare) I more or less dragged the peer downstairs whispering words of encouragement during the unhurryable performance. "As soon as you can my Lord", "The President is a little anxious Sir".

He took me well, saying with a smile "You don't mind if I closhe my zip old boy" which made me laugh aloud and forgive him everything, and then we made haste to join the procession.

As he took his place alongside the President he swayed slightly, causing a ripple of apprehension among those learned V.I.P's and a strangled scream from the President. Could our Principal Guest be pickled?

We had to get the banquet going, however, so I took the Procession to the entrance of the banqueting hall and announcing, "Be pleased to receive the President and your Principal Guests", marched them in to the acclamation of the great assembly.

The journey from door to top table was very interesting. I saw guest after guest slowly stop clapping as we approached, stare at the Guest of Honour behind me and then whisper to neighbours. "He's p…" I could see their lips move…

On reaching the top table and positioning the President and his Lordship in their places, I called for silence for "Grace, by the President" and was interested to note that our peer was holding on to the back of his chair, as if for support.

As everyone sat down the waitress having, as normal, quietly asked me to point out the President and the Guest of Honour, proceeded to serve them.

"I don't want anything to eat, Sweetie", said the Guest of Honour "just bring me a bottle of wine".

With that he swept his knives, forks and spoon, wine glasses and side plate away, crossed one arm over the other on the table, placed his head upon them and fell asleep.

The President's face at this stage was a picture; this was his great night and his principal speaker looked as though he was going to spend it in a drunken stupor. Amid the great buzz of conversation, the clatter of plates, the disapproving glances of the V.I.P's there he was, fast asleep. (Personally it made me giggle).

The meal proceeded of course – it had to – with the poor President assuming an ever more gloomy countenance, very occasionally attempting to open a conversation with the Right Honourable 'log' on his left but never receiving more than a grunt for his pains.

Round about the start of the sweet course I whispered into the President's right ear, "I've been with his Lordship before, Sir, and he may yet surprise us; but in case we can't wake him up, would another of your guests consider saying a few words at short notice?"

There was no response. The poor chap was just sitting there, shell-shocked.

"Mr President" I said in a louder voice and clinking his spoon against an empty glass, "Mr President, I've been with this chap before and he was alright in the end but in case he isn't, have you someone who can fill in?"

The President turned, nearly rejoined the living and, with face twitching like the police superintendent in The Pink Panther films, stammered, "I don't know, I don't know". He then went back into his trance.

I decided to concentrate upon the Guest of Honour and a few minutes later, at the 'clear' of the Sweet course, shook him quite firmly and hissed "My Lord we're just about to propose the Loyal Toast".

For good measure I then banged the table three times with my gavel close to his right ear to announce the Loyal Toast. He stood for this, swaying gently glass raised in right hand with left hand gripping the table for support. Good; at least we could get him on to his feet!

Coffee was soon served and then it was time for the great man to speak. "I'll be calling upon you to address the guests in a moment, my Lord", I breathed. "Will that be alright Sir?"

"Shirtainly, ole boy" was the response "fire away".

So I gavelled up and announced to a room suddenly and startlingly silent. It wouldn't be an exaggeration to say that the atmosphere was electric.

The ever surprising peer then rose and delivered a very lucid and coherent address, describing in detail to a spellbound audience how, having failed over many years to win a seat in Parliament, the Communist Party had strongly infiltrated the unions and the Labour party itself, with disastrous consequences for the country.

He sat down after twenty minutes to great applause and felt free to engage in a little carefree drinking until the conclusion of the final speech. He then suddenly told us he was leaving and started to do so.

Hurriedly proclaiming "Please stand to honour the departure of your Principal Guest" I lead him in a lurch through the now cheering throng, out to the reception hall and then in a long stagger toward the exit.

My chauffeur was coming towards us and I hissed to her, "Be with you in a minute, Rosie..."

"Roshie? Who'sh Roshie?" demanded his Lordship.

"My wife, Sir" explained the long suffering Toastmaster, "Come to take me home". "Rosie, meet Lord ..."

Rosie got a quick bear-hug and what she later described as the sloppiest kiss of her life (aimed at her lips but by good footwork on her part diverted to her cheek) and we were again meandering toward the exit.

The commissionaire was missing so I called a taxi over from the rank. "Cabbie" I started to confide, "I've got old Lord ... here. Will you take him where he..."

Whoosh! The taxi was gone, leaving the nice man in the red coat and his tipsy friend in the roadway looking very puzzled indeed.

I hailed another taxi and this time more sensibly first opened the door and helped our friend to fall in before speaking to the cabbie.

"My pal's had a few, chum" I said cheerfully "but he's alright for a good tip and he'll tell you where he lives".

"O.K. boss" answered the cabbie "I'll take care of 'im. Move 'im in an close the door, will ya?"

My 'pal' was still kneeling on the cab floor with his rear-end protruding into the night. One push on the baronly bottom and I was able to shut the door – and the taxi was off.

You know that feeling of relief when you take a long unwanted article to the Council tip and just throw it?

Walking slowly back to Rosie and taking some very deep breaths indeed, I was stopped by an anxious Spanish cloakroom attendant. "Senor" she gasped, "your friend, 'ee forget 'ees coat".

Rest in peace, my Lord.

136

89. Movement study

Since early youth I've tried to train myself to be observant. These days I wonder if I've been wise; one can see and hear *too* much.

I've used Toastmastering as an aid to observation and memory. Noting a person's mode of dress, height, features, name or even strength of voice when you announce him, helps you to find him later in a crowd when he is due to give a speech, and to know how high and how near to set the microphone for him. If you remember too that he's left-handed and also deaf in the right ear, you can save him and yourself possible embarrassment.

Having the opportunity to meet very many people also makes it easier to spot different types of 'workers' and I was once complimented at the Savoy for apparently being able to pick out, at some ten yards range, guests for the different parties and, before they could say a word, direct them to the right room for their party.

"American Bar Association, Sir?" – "In the Lincoln Room three flights down".

"Jockeys' Benevolent Society – third door on the right, Sir".

"Israeli Charity Committee Madam? Iolanthe Room through that archway, please"

"Bankers' party, Mr Marshall? This way, Sir".

"Pop Record Company – Lancaster Room, keeping going that way, Sir."

"Ladies' Powder Room at the end of the passage, Madam" (this in a whisper).

Thinking about it, I realised that I knew the Americans from their close cropped hair and 'half-mast' trousers; the Jockeys from their lean, small, bow-legged look; the Israeli Charity lady and her committee from their mink coats and diamonds; the banker from his short hair and dark suit (he was also from The Bank); the Pop Record Company men from their very 'with-it' outfits and not a tie among them, and the lady who wanted the Powder Room from the general demeanour – especially the blush.

Not very clever really, but now that I am aware of people watching me, I tend to show off a bit. Which reminds me of the visit to Britain of the Sydney Philharmonic Orchestra and the Sydney Ballet Company when a party was given in their honour at Australia House by the High Commissioner.

His Excellency asked me to announce the name of each guest and the organisation he represented. There were to be many theatre and television executives attending and he wanted to be able to have a short conversation with each about their job – as they arrived.

After a succession of terribly, terribly English theatre managers, B.B.C. producers and the like, I saw an untidy, portly figure approaching. He had lips like Louis Armstrong, egg stain on his tie, and crumpled trousers. As he told me his name I detected an 'Austrylian' accent.

'And you're a member of the Orchestra, Sir?"

"Why-er, yes" he said, with an appreciative glance. "that's good".

Next came a tall athletic chap in a very light suit. He bounced up and down on his toes as he walked towards me, his stiff fair hair looking like a TV commercial for shampoo. He answered my question, "May I have your name, Sir?" in a high tenor Aussie voice, "Garth Windsor".

"And *you're* a member of the ballet, Sir"

He was astonished. "I say, that's extremely clever of you" he murmured.

It wasn't really.

90. The whip off

I enjoy giving my wife little surprises – it helps keep the marriage exciting. She likes surprises too – most of the time.

One night after a Charity Banquet the Duchess of Gloucester was preparing to leave when the Committee asked if they could present to her a few of the handicapped people in whose aid the Charity was being run.

She of course readily agreed but asked me if I would collect her stole from the cloakroom, to save time later.

As you can imagine, it was a stole of the most beautiful fur and many women in the foyer looked at it rather lovingly as I carried it through (or where they looking at me? – I'll never know).

While I'd been in the cloakroom my wife had arrived in the foyer. One look at that familiar figure gave me an idea... I crept up behind her and placed the gorgeous stole gently round the neck of my favourite gal.

She turned slowly, muzzling the fur against her cheek, stroking it with her hands. "Oh Ben" she breathed, "Ben ... you shouldn't have ..."

With one quick whip the stole was off ... as so was dear Ben!

"You silly Moo" I called back, "It's the Duchess of Gloucester's".

She always reckoned she had grounds for a divorce.

91. Smiling relief or incident in the early morn.

Whilst our Landing Ship Tank was waiting in the north eastern Italian port of Ancona during the clear-up at the end of the War in Europe, I went down to the open bow doors and out along the ramp for a bit of fresh air and to see if there was any sign of the fleet of army lorries which we were to take to Trieste, where our liberating armies, under Field Marshal Alexander were having some trouble with Yugo-Slav forces who thought they should be allowed to take over that lovely town.

I felt pretty jaded at that moment. I'd been Officer of the Watch that night, covering the return to the ship of drunken liberty men and had also been called upon to put a stop to some nefarious goings on round the stern of the ship where a filthy Italian fisherman was selling his smelly wife's services to some of our sailors in a small rowing boat, the inside of which was covered in sticky fish scales! There were times I despaired over Jolly Jack Tar!

Then something happened which brightened me up considerably and planted a life long memory in my young brain. Across the vast dockside there suddenly came the sound of military commands and heavy beat of marching feet. Then there came into view the ultra

keen, proud and upright South West African Zulu Infantry – the famous "SWARZIS". They were there in a stevedoring role, unloading the military supply ships.

It always thrills me to see such fine men marching so proudly and they really held my attention.

Suddenly, on the loud commands "Halt" and "Dismiss", they broke off and rushed towards our ship. As they neared the ramp they split right and left, forming a line along the quayside on either side of our bows. It must have been a long march because they all then immediately relieved themselves.

The sight of these hundred or so stalwart men with their exposed and considerable manhood's raised a great laugh amongst we Navy boys on the ramp and, upon hearing this the great line of jet black faces broke into yard wide, flashing smiles!

What a sight to savour. If only I'd had a camera … . But I hadn't, and the moment had gone for ever.

Perhaps not however, now that I've penned this little memory.

92. Finders weepers

Man and boy I've always been finding things. Maybe I get this gift from my dear old Mum who once retraced my mile and a half journey back from school and found the tiny winding button I'd lost from my brand new wristwatch.

I've actually found and returned thousands of pounds worth of other people's possessions. Rings worth £7,000 and £800; wallets worth £6,000 and £500; a purse containing £109; cash amounts of £156, £60, £50, £16, £5 etc. also cheque-books and credit cards. Also incidentally a few hundred four leafed clovers too, in six different countries.

Finding something valuable, returning it to a distraught owner, being thanked or even rewarded should be an enjoyable experience; sadly, in most cases, the opposite seems true.

When I found the £7,000 ring, for instance, during the Cocktail Reception prior to a firm's Dinner/Dance at the Criterion Restaurant and guessed it could only have been dropped by the wife of the millionaire Chairman, I very quietly returned it to her; but not quietly enough to escape the fox-like ear of her monstrous, bullying giant of a husband who, as I was handing the ring to her, spun round, grabbed it and screamed, "That's a seven thousand pound ring, you stupid cow! Where's the other one?"

Thirty years later, I still await even "thank you," and during that period the same thing has happened time and time again; I find something, go to a lot of trouble to return it to its owner – and don't get thanked.

The worst case, I think, was when my wife and I were taking a romantic, after midnight stroll around the promenade deck of a cruise liner in the Mediterranean. A supremely happy day had just finished with ballroom-dancing, which we both love, and now here I was, arm round the gal I adore, marvelling at the full moon dancing on the tiny waves ...

Suddenly, unromantically and to her annoyance, I was off. My eyes, temporarily straying from the moonlight sea had wandered inboard, through the entrance of the "Gents," across its floor, into an open cubicle and past the toilet where on the deck, near the "S" bend, they'd espied a great, fat, black wallet.

Within seconds I'd retrieved it and found it was crammed with high denomination English and foreign bank notes, travellers' cheques and credit cards.

For a streetwise kid out of Hoxton the next step was blindingly obvious; whip out the untraceable notes and chuck the rest of the evidence overboard.

Some candle within me, lit perhaps during my service in the Bank, however, guided my footsteps back to the Ballroom where I'd earlier noted the 1st Mate, the Chief Engineer and the Chief Purser settling down for a well-earned drink.

They gave weary sighs as we approached them ...

"Chief," I said to the Purser, "I'm sorry to interrupt ..." "Can't it wait till the morning Sir?" he breathed, "This is our first break in twenty-six hours." "I think I know exactly how you're feeling, gents" I apologised, "I'm an old sailor myself; but I've just found some chap's wallet with all his money for the whole of the cruise. He and his family will be frantic, they'll have no sleep tonight."

"I can't start making announcements at nearly one o'clock in the morning" he started to protest ...

"What about searching the wallet for his identity, looking him up in the Passenger List and giving me his cabin number" I ventured. "Come on Chief – imagine if you'd lost everything on the first night of your cruise ..."

He looked at his shipmates, gave a deep sigh and took us off to his office. Rummaging through the wallet he said, "There's about £6,000 in cash, alone, here" and redoubled his efforts.

Suddenly he called, "I know this name, he's on the ship! Wait a sec., there he is. Cabin 142. Can I get back to my drink now, Sir?"

"Thanks very much Chief" we said and shot off, happy with the thought that we were about to re-unite a man and his precious holiday money; perhaps even prevent his wife strangling him.

I think it was about a quarter past one when, all excited, we tapped on the door of Cabin 142, near the "Gents."

"What the hell do you want?" came a very nasty, snarling voice.

We looked at each other and for one teeny weenie fraction of a second I considered the Hoxton alternative; but the Bank's candle still glowed within me.

"Excuse us" I called "sorry to disturb you. We think we've found something you may have lost…" The door was suddenly wrenched open, an arm shot out and a hand grabbed the wallet from my friendly, caring grasp. The door was then slammed shut.

"It's happened again, Ben!" gasped my shell-shocked wife. "I didn't even see his face" I spluttered, as she led me away, dazed and furious.

It took a couple of angry, waiting, frustrated days before I was able to trace and tackle the occupant of Cabin 142, in a queue for tea. "Excuse me" I said fairly aggressively, "are you the gentleman whose wallet I found a couple of nights ago?" "Oh, yes" he replied, "I meant to thank you …"

Meant to thank me! I'd saved the b…'s holiday! At this stage the Bank's candle went out and I reverted to Hoxtonian phrases. Quite enjoyable too, but not as satisfactory as a nice "Thank you" would have been on the night.

My next memorable find was the purse with the £109 in it. It was a black one, lying in the road in Eltham Well Hall and cars were running over it.

An examination of the purse on our arrival home set us on a search for a Mrs. Muldane, who appeared either to work for, or to receive benefits from the Social Security Department. It transpired that she worked there and the authorities, while unwilling to give me her address or telephone number, agreed to ask her to ring me.

When she did so and I told her I thought I'd found something of hers, she said, in a strong Irish brogue "Would it be a black purse with £109 in it?" Game set and match.

She'd apparently dropped it as she stepped from a late night taxi a few minutes before I drove by.

We arranged that I should return it to her on my way up to London that evening. It would mean my double parking in a very busy road at 5.30 p.m. but she was there exactly on time and her head was soon poked through the passenger window.

"Mister Soollivan?" she enquired. "Mrs. Muldane" I presumed, "Here's your purse dear. Would you like to check it?"

"Thertainly not" came the emphatic reply, "and this is for you."

It was a ten pound note! I was overwhelmed. After all these years someone was really showing gratitude. Choked, I pushed the note back. "I won't take it, sweetheart," I started to say, "but you'll never know how grateful I am for the offer …"

The note was pushed back to me. "Take it. TAKE IT" insisted a fierce Mrs. Muldane.

I had a fierce Irish mother myself, so I took it and later bought ten Premium Savings Bonds with the prayer that one day I'd win on one of them and send half the prize to the lady who'd restored my faith in human nature.

Further restoration came last year when, in pouring rain, I found a lorry driver's wallet in City Road which contained a (to him, priceless) plastic card issued by the Inland Revenue which enabled him to be paid in cash for loads he delivered to building sites. Without it his living was gone as it is not the Revenue's policy to replace lost cards.

141

Having got his name and address from his Driving Licence and his telephone number from Directory Enquiries, I phoned him from the Portman Hotel where I was going to work that evening.

He was so thrilled about it that he came straight to the hotel, by lorry, in his (very) rough togs and joined the long line of gorgeously dressed Italian men and women that I was announcing to their bank President.

When this apparition finally appeared before me, he panted "I'm Gary Platt. Your name Sullivan?"

Startled out of my wits, I gasped "Blimey" and opened my red coat wide so that he could see the long black wallet sticking out of my inside pocket. He snatched it with his left hand (memories of the cruise!) but then, with a swing of his right hand, presented me with a litre bottle of whisky, Then shot off … .

Three cheers for the working class!

Note

As I started to put these recollections to paper, you've guessed it, I found some more money! £50 – sticking out of a Cash Dispenser in the Strand.

Telephoning the bank I was informed that they'd had an enquiry from a customer who'd drawn £50 cash but couldn't find it. They said they weren't allowed to give me his name, nor give him mine, but could I send my cheque made out to them so that they could credit his account. I did so, and have heard no more. Nor will I.

Here we go again ?